ALFIE'S WAR

A sequel to *Seven Seas, Nine Lives* –
more war experiences of
Captain A W F 'Alfie' Sutton CBE DSC* RN

ALFIE'S WAR

A FLEET AIR ARM OFFICER'S EXCITING EXPLOITS ON HMS *ILLUSTRIOUS*, IN GREECE AND CRETE

Richard Pike

Richard Pike (signature)

Grub Street • London

Published by
Grub Street Publishing
4 Rainham Close
London
SW11 6SS

Copyright © Grub Street 2012
Copyright text © Richard Pike 2012

British Library Cataloguing in Publication Data
Pike, Richard, 1943-
   Alfie's War: A Fleet Air Arm Officer's exciting exploits on
   HMS *Illustrious*, in Greece and Crete.
   1. Sutton, A. W. F. (Alan William Frank)
   2. Great Britain. Royal Navy. Fleet Air Arm–History.
   3. World War, 1939-1945–Naval operations, British.
   I. Title
   940.5'45'941'092-dc23

ISBN-13: 9781908117410

Edited by Sophie Campbell

Book design and artwork by Roy Platten, Eclipse
roy.eclipse@btopenworld.com

Printed and bound by MPG Ltd, Bodmin, Cornwall

Grub Street Publishing uses only FSC (Forest Stewardship
Council) paper for its books.

Publisher's Note: Captain A W F 'Alfie' Sutton referred to himself
as the lieutenant, and we have kept this style throughout.

Contents

Preface

German snipers started to move in. They were backed by a number of mortar units which began systematically to attack the whole of the hillside. They would work their way up and down the hill, then across, then up and down again. We could see the mortar bombs coming; it was a case of grabbing one's rifle then rolling down the hill to take up a new position out of the way of the exploding bombs.

After a period of this routine, eventually I found myself behind a pack of discarded Royal Marine equipment: pairs of boots; a military greatcoat; and a number of backpacks. I decided to try and scoop a defensive trench in this spot. I had to make use of my Royal Air Force-issued tin hat although it was pretty tough going: the ground was hard and the tin hat made a less than perfect tool. Even so, I managed to dig a reasonable trench although, as I was digging, I began to realise that the red, white and blue of the Royal Air Force roundel on the front of the tin hat provided an ideal aiming bulls-eye for the enemy. I hastily erased the roundel which was just as well since snipers were beginning to make things very difficult.

I found myself in a duel with a particular sniper. I knew where he was, although he had made a decoy which he hoped I would aim at. Every time he fired, I fired back. His bullets hit the Royal Marine equipment and we kept this up for some time. Eventually, as it was getting towards late afternoon and as I knew that it would become very cold overnight, I attempted to retrieve the Royal Marine greatcoat. Every time I moved, a hail of two or three bullets would hit the Royal Marine pack. In spite of this, I was able to ease the greatcoat out of its pack very slowly, although the bloody sniper thwarted my efforts to recover the boots, and I realised I would be stuck with my thin officer's shoes if I managed to escape.

As evening approached, the Royal Marines managed to get their anti-aircraft guns operational again and this brought down a special form of hate from the Luftwaffe. Enemy pilots launched an intense air attack against Hill 107. So powerful, in fact, that they set fire to the top of the hill: undergrowth; stores; ammunition all went up in a massive blaze. I therefore found myself pinned down between the sniper and the conflagration at the top of the hill, not a comfortable situation. However, as dusk fell, I was finally able to extricate myself under the cover of darkness. It was then that a message came round that we were to withdraw to an area further up the hillside....

Hill 107, Maleme, Crete, 20th May 1941

PART ONE

Illustrious Blitz

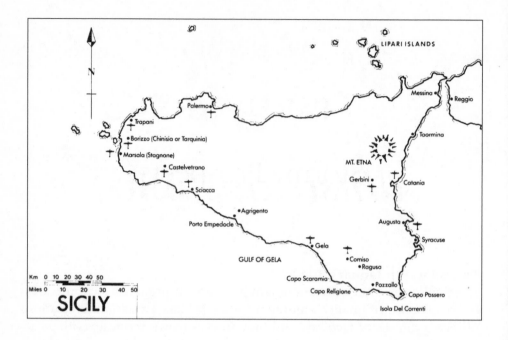

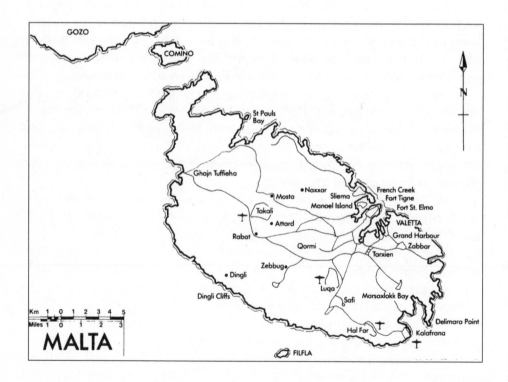

1

Stormy Prospects

Thursday, 9th January 1941

The news is greeted with a poignant hush and apprehensive expressions betray a sense of finality. Lieutenant Alan William Frank ('Alfie') Sutton observes the sea of faces around him and his frown replicates others as he notes the lingering aura of silence, the air of discomfiture, with those present unwilling to be rushed into comment. The quiet spell is accentuated by the steady throb of machinery as men listen to the distant hum of the aircraft carrier's Parson's turbines. When Lieutenant Sutton glances at his colleague seated nearby, he notes the officer's sober expression, so uncharacteristic of his normally ebullient manner.

He returns his gaze to the commander in front. The commander, who stands and faces the officers to brief those not on watch or other immediate duty, has attempted to sound measured in his approach. However, those who know him well recognise that the senior officer's awareness of moment and his turmoil of emotion have been betrayed by the occasional waver of his tone.

Now, those gathered in the wardroom seem uncertain how to react. Some officers look down, others glance upwards at the wardroom deck-head, a few stare blankly at their hands. All seem anxious to avoid letting slip their thoughts. Perhaps the men even fear the embarrassment of an inappropriate outburst. If women were present, thinks Sutton, the atmosphere would be different; there might even be the sound of nervous whispering in the background. Perhaps the female reaction would be less reserved, and more willing to reveal sentiments, recognition of how their situation has been drastically, alarmingly, transformed.

The commander makes a nervous gesture with one hand. "So that, gentlemen," he says tersely, "will present us, I'm afraid, with a wholly different situation." He hesitates and wipes his brow. Others do the same as if made suddenly conscious of the intensity of atmosphere created by the ship's air conditioning system. "From now on we'll have to contend with an adversary of greater significance – *far* greater – than in the past."

"Do we know, sir," asks one of the pilots, "when these German squadrons are likely to be declared fully operational?"

"Captain Boyd is painfully aware of the sketchy nature of official intelligence, however we've made assumptions based on our own observations and on those of local contacts in Malta. It seems, though, that the Admiralty and the Air Ministry staff are convinced that the presence of the Luftwaffe will make little difference to the threat already posed by the Italian Regia Aeronautica. Whether the staff in London are trying to put a brave face on things," he shrugs, "who knows? I think that most of us here – and surely most others in the Mediterranean Fleet – appreciate a different reality. It could be a mere matter of days, as the captain has suggested, before the Germans start to launch attacks, especially as we draw closer to Malta."

The commander's remarks are followed by a resumption of the wardroom's uncomfortable hush. The silence is broken eventually by a midshipman who half stands to ask: "Is there, maybe, another aspect, sir…?"

"Speak up, mister," interjects the commander; he points briskly with one finger towards the midshipman at the far end of the room.

"I just meant to ask, sir…" the midshipman falters again, his anxiety apparent. All eyes in the room now turn hastily, impatiently, to observe the young man who struggles to sound coherent. Lieutenant Sutton feels sudden commiseration, a mix of sympathy and embarrassment, for the questioner and his predicament. He decides – as if to help assuage the blushes of the midshipman – to avert his gaze; he glances instead at a picture placed prominently on an adjacent bulkhead.

The photograph, he recalls, was taken last year during the ship's operational work up in Bermuda. His Majesty's Ship *Illustrious*, the Royal Navy's newest and most technically-advanced aircraft carrier, can be seen at her impressive best. With a sense of admiration, he focuses on the image, the distinctive form of the ship's profile, the tidy trenches carved by her hull before the seas collapse in a chaos of froth. Amassed astern, great waves are churned by her propulsion system. He can make out varieties of naval aircraft ranged on the *Illustrious*'s flight deck, a mix of Fairey Fulmars and his own aircraft type, the Fairey Swordfish.

As he continues to stare at the photograph, the spirit of camaraderie within the ship's company is almost tangible. The men are invigorated by the Bermudan sunshine, individuals determined to play their part to hone the potential of this recent and vital addition to the country's war effort. He becomes absorbed in thought. The midshipman's predicament – his shrill voice – appears to fade into the distance as, with his mind stirred after the commander's comments, the lieutenant starts to reflect on his own role and how his background has led to his present situation on the *Illustrious*.

During his early days in the navy, as a young midshipman he was forced to witness the unrest of ratings at the Invergordon mutiny ten years ago, in September 1931. The ordeal may have marked his formative days, but his enthusiasm for a naval career remained undimmed. His turbulent introduction to naval life (on the battle-cruiser HMS *Repulse*) had been followed by a series of postings on destroyers as he developed his skills in the executive branch of the Royal Navy. By the late 1930s, when he had gained sufficient experience for a key ship's role, he was assigned as second lieutenant to HMS *Basilisk*.

The *Basilisk*, a twin-turbine destroyer of 1,360-ton displacement and capable of speeds up to thirty-five knots, had been part of an international arrangement required to patrol the Bilbao-Santander coast during the Spanish Civil War. He remembers how the patrol routines, inclined to repetitive dreariness, had assumed sudden excitement when the captain ordered an armed party to board a suspicious-looking merchantman. He has other memories too: the opportunities when the ship was off-duty, the pleasurable days in harbour at Saint-Jean-de-Luz, the relaxation afforded by sun and sand in southern France, not least the curious circumstances that had led to a chance encounter with a young woman who would become his wife. From then on there was a need for determined ingenuity in order to fit his naval duties around his romantic ones.

Lieutenant Sutton ruminates how his situation had typified the age-old predicaments of the seafarer, with all the dilemmas of a life at sea. He ponders the differences, so stark, between the conditions on the *Basilisk* and those on the *Illustrious*. The large ship may offer comforts and amenities denied to crews on smaller vessels, but, nonetheless, life on the carrier could lack the character – the challenges – of destroyers. Both types, though have remained equally exposed to the dangers of enemy action, and the vagaries of the elements.

There was an incident last summer when the *Illustrious* had faced violent storms as she crossed the Bay of Biscay during sea trials en-route to Bermuda for her work up. The episode was recalled later by a seaman in the ship's news digest:

'We hit heavy weather as soon as we entered the Bay of Biscay. The seas ran so high that the fo'c's'le (forecastle) deck was continuously awash as the *Illustrious* dipped through the troughs and then rode the swells. At times the waves nearly came over the flight deck. All around, gear was smashed. Scuttles and dead-lights, meant to seal portholes to darken the ship, and for heavy weather, were smashed in. The shipwrights had a very busy time.'

The description is similar to an even more hazardous crossing of the Bay of Biscay, when he was on duty on HMS *Basilisk*. In the extreme conditions, the *Basilisk*'s 1360 tons had compared unfavourably with the 23,000-ton displacement of the *Illustrious*. As the wind's strength had escalated to storm force on the beam, shelter for the *Basilisk*'s crew had proved increasingly illusive. Men had listened with alarm to the creaks and groans from superstructure, the wail of the wind, and the drone of ventilation fans – eerily hollow – as they drew air towards the ship's interior.

Officers on the bridge had to roar their orders while the steering gear struggled to hold the *Basilisk*'s course. The wind's howl, as if afflicted by some demoniac hysteria, rose to a shriek. Water snatched from the wave crests was hurled against the bridge and forecastle. Spray as solid as streamers lashed against oilskins before heading for scuppers in a rush of grumbles and gurgles. The unfortunate crewmen whose duties forced them outside slithered along drenched decks; men winced at the scour of spray thrown up by the seas, and the sting of salt against faces and hands. Half-closed eyes, as they squinted aft, observed the plumes powered high by the screws, the ferocious furrows along the sea's surface. As individuals battled to meet the ship's motion, all were compelled to grab for the nearest handrail or stanchion.

Once, when a crest towered out of the blackness to windward, a high wall of water struck with exceptional vigour. The wave shattered its bulk against the *Basilisk*'s broadside; from stem to stern, the ship shuddered with shock. A leading seaman, as he wrestled with loosened lashings, was caught wrong-footed. His cry of pain – masked by the wind's screech – went unheeded as he persisted with his task, now hampered by a fingernail torn from his finger.

Another crew member, who had to shake his head to clear blood from a wound above his eyes, swayed dizzily on the slippery surfaces. Personal traumas, though, had to be endured with stoicism. The minutes seemed endless, and the hours eternal; men lost track of time. It seemed the sea's onslaught would never end but eventually, at around dawn, the blackness of ragged clouds driven up from the south-west began to lighten. The thoughts of better times, the cheer of an open fire, the body of a pin-up girl, sleep in a warm, still bed, were buoyed by hot cocoa and soup brought up from the galley. At last, the vexation of crew members could be eased.

Lieutenant Sutton recalls such experiences with nostalgia but with them come the strong sense of achievement, and that of fulfilment. As an intrepid individual, he has relished the stimulation of life at sea. Nonetheless, after his time on the *Basilisk* and when the Royal Navy career system required him to choose a specialist branch, he had decided to seek new challenges. So it was that he opted to volunteer in 1937 for the up-and-coming Fleet Air Arm, by then in the process of separation from the Royal Air Force as the country prepared for war.

His initial aircrew training was carried out at Ford, a grass airfield near Arundel in Sussex. The airfield, re-commissioned as part of air force expansion plans, was used as the base for the School of Naval Co-operation of the Royal Air Force. Posted there in January 1938 as a member of 32 Naval Observer's Course, he joined six fellow Royal Naval officers and two officers from the Royal Air Force. The course members learned the arts of air reconnaissance, fleet auxiliary work, and navigation.

One of the instructors at Ford was an academic type who impressed upon the budding observers that they should become adept at 'dead reckoning' techniques in order to navigate successfully over the sea. The bespectacled instructor, a keen mathematician, caused a buzz of discussion amongst the students when he declared:

"When in rudimentary situations, I'd like to suggest the need to apply fundamental principles. When in doubt, go back to basics. Think of the methods used by the great logicians: Pythagoras; Philolaus ('all things that are known have a number'); Euclid, the latter's thirteen books on geometry and arithmetic. Remember how, to this day – over 2,000 years later – Euclid's books are still used as standard works of reference."

"Can you expand on that, please?" asked one of the students, perhaps about to regret his outburst.

"Certainly, young man. Think of this: any straight line can be infinitely extended. And this: it is possible to describe a circle with any centre and any radius. And this: our present decimal numerals are based on a Hindu-Arabic system."

"Thank you, sir."

"And the following principle can be especially useful: if a straight line falling on two straight lines makes the interior angles on the same side less than two right angles, the straight lines, if produced indefinitely, will meet on that side on which the angles are less than the two right angles.

Gentlemen: when all else fails – for instance, on a dark and dirty night, far from land and aircraft carrier and when, in both senses of the expression, you find yourselves completely at sea – think about Euclid and try to apply his principles."

Some four years have elapsed since his aircrew training, and now aged twenty-nine he is a fully-qualified and experienced Fleet Air Arm observer. However, the lieutenant still remembers the excitement of his early flying, especially the exhilaration of adding a new dimension to his naval career, and the thrill of the training flights at Ford performed on the Blackburn Shark, an adapted torpedo spotter/reconnaissance biplane.

At the end of his six-month course at Ford, in June 1938 he was posted as an observer on Swordfish aircraft and based on the aircraft carrier HMS *Glorious* in the Mediterranean theatre. The period was an unfortunate one, a time of opportunities wasted, enthusiasm squandered – a difficult time for him personally, and for the Fleet Air Arm branch as a whole. Certain traditionalists had tended to treat Fleet Air Arm members with suspicion, even refusing conversation if they saw a particular individual as inclined to dilute the status of officer. The situation on HMS *Glorious* had not been helped by the presence of an awkward, cantankerous captain disposed to squabble with his fellow officers, especially senior members of the Fleet Air Arm.

Lieutenant Sutton's eighteen or so months on the *Glorious* had seen the morale of her crew decline progressively and he had been relieved, therefore, to be posted away from an unhappy ship. He was glad to be appointed, in January 1940, to another Swordfish unit, 819 Squadron, destined for embarkation on HMS *Illustrious* at the completion of the carrier's construction in the spring of that year. In addition to his own squadron, the *Illustrious* would operate another Swordfish unit (815 Squadron) and one fighter squadron (806 Squadron), equipped with Fairey Fulmars.

He is now one of the Fleet Air Arm's more experienced Swordfish observers and, as a consequence, he has learned to view his aircraft with particular esteem. Popularly known as the 'Stringbag', the Swordfish's obsolete appearance belies the machine's unexpected qualities of handling and robustness. Last November, when some twenty Swordfish were used to attack the Italian Fleet in harbour at Taranto, the aircrew had achieved spectacular results despite the anti-aircraft efforts (similarly impressive) thrown up by the enemy.

The survival of the majority of the aircrews had been, in part, thanks to the rugged nature of their aircraft. After the attack, Lieutenant Sutton and his pilot, Lieutenant 'Tiffy' Torrens-Spence, had been awarded

Distinguished Service Crosses in recognition of their bravery and tenacity in pressing their torpedo attack against an enemy battleship. Later, they had learned how the handful of Swordfish had achieved more damage to the enemy than the combined efforts of the British Grand Fleet at Jutland, with all of that battle's terrible losses.

He reflects on the Stringbag's properties, how these had helped to bring about such results. Powered by a single 690 horsepower Bristol Pegasus 111M or a single 750 horsepower Pegasus XXX engine, the Fairey Swordfish could carry combinations of torpedoes, mines, or depth charges. The aircraft, armed with a fixed, synchronised Browning machine-gun forward, a Lewis or Vickers 'K' gun aft, normally would carry a crew of three in open cockpits. The aircraft's exceptional handling characteristics would be summarised by one pilot thus:

'You could pull a Swordfish off the deck and put her in a climbing turn at fifty-five knots. A steep turn at sea level towards the attacker just before he came within range and the difference in speed and the small turning circle made it impossible for the fighter to bring its guns to bear for more than a few seconds. The approach to the carrier deck could be made at staggeringly slow speed, yet response to the controls remained firm and insistent. Consider what such qualities meant on a dark night when the carrier's deck was pitching the height of a house.'

The Swordfish, which entered service in July 1936, is due to be replaced by the new Fairey Albacore, another biplane but with improved performance and fitted with closed cockpits. However, in time, the older aircraft's qualities will mean she outlives her intended successor, and that the last of the 2,932 Swordfish to be produced will retire in July 1945. He ruminates that the Albacore is powered by a notoriously unreliable Bristol Taurus engine whose quirks have been captured by a recent entry in the Fleet Air Arm song book:

(Sung to the tune of 'My Bonnie lies over the ocean')

The Swordfish relies on her Peggy
The tinny Taurus, it just ain't sound
So the Swordfish flies off on her missions
And the Albacore stays on the ground
Bring back, bring back
Oh bring back my Stringbag to me...

"Sorry, sir, just a thought…" the lieutenant's reminiscences are interrupted when he picks up the shrill tones of the midshipman again. The young officer sits down, but his mood remains fretful. The commander, no doubt aware that the midshipman's unease reflects the wardroom's general air of tension, is conscious, nonetheless, of the need to point out necessary facts. He decides to introduce another speaker:

"It might be appropriate for me to ask our Royal Air Force liaison officer to say a word or two at this juncture," says the commander. He searches around the room.

"Yes, sir," says the flight lieutenant, standing up.

"Thank you, flight lieutenant. Perhaps you could offer a recap of the updated air threat."

"Certainly, sir," says the flight lieutenant.

"As most of us know by now, Luftwaffe units have been observed as they moved south from Poland over the last few days. We believe the corps involved is the Tenth Air Corps, Fliegerkorps X, commanded by General Geissler. Although at this point we're unclear exactly how the general will use his squadrons, we think their role is likely to be restricted to one of support for the Italian Regia Aeronautica.

"We believe that Sicily will be the main base for the Luftwaffe units and that Malta will thus become a prime target for attack. As the commander has just indicated, we can expect the German squadrons to be powerful and efficient. From intelligence summaries, we know the Tenth Air Corps to be one of the Luftwaffe's premier units, with an estimated 150 Heinkel 111 and Junkers Ju 88 medium bombers, the same number of Junkers Ju 87 Stuka dive-bombers, and fifty Messerschmitt Bf 109 fighters."

"So which type," asks a member of aircrew, "is most likely to be used in attacks against us?"

"It could be any or all of these types, though the renowned accuracy of the Stukas makes that aircraft ideal for anti-shipping strikes."

"Are there any more details?"

"We believe the Tenth Air Corps has some experienced anti-shipping crews. Up to now the Germans have relied on the likes of the long-range Focke-Wulf Fw 200 Condors and the Junkers Ju 290s for anti-shipping activities in the North Atlantic. Over Mediterranean waters, however, the infamous tactics of the Stukas can be employed. This will present us with a formidable threat."

"Will our Fulmar fighters be able to cope?"

"The Stuka is a sturdy and accurate machine, but the aircraft has significant limitations." The flight lieutenant glances at the commander. "Would you like me to cover a few facts and figures, sir?"

"Please refresh our memories."

"An attacking Stuka has the ability to hold an accurate dive of up to eighty degrees. The Ju 87B-1 version has a maximum speed of just over 200 miles per hour, a ceiling of around 25,000 feet, but a weak point is the machine's range: limited to some 350 miles or so. The Stuka's armament consists of three 7.9-mm machine guns, and various combinations of bombs/torpedoes can be fitted. The manufacturers have devised an automatic pull-up system to ensure the machine's recovery from a steep dive, even if high 'g' forces have caused the pilot to black out.

"A well-known and unattractive feature of the Stuka is the wail created by special sirens, a noise designed to produce an unnerving effect and to shatter morale.

"In summary, gentlemen, the Stuka presents us with a powerful opponent but one with certain distinct limitations. The machine's slowness and lack of manoeuvrability make it especially vulnerable when confronted by our Fulmars and other fighters."

"Thank you, flight lieutenant," says the commander. He checks his watch.

"I think we'll have to wrap it up there, gentlemen. Before long, the ship is due to reach a position some 200 miles east-south-east of Malta. Operation Excess will proceed as planned: we'll continue to sail westwards and our rendezvous with the convoy from Gibraltar should take place tomorrow as intended. The fleet's defences will remain robust; the Regia Aeronautica will be on the prowl and, as the captain has warned us, we can anticipate Luftwaffe intervention quite soon. However, this shouldn't happen, hopefully, for a day or so yet. I don't think any of us," he glances at the midshipman, "should overreact." He hesitates before asking: "Are there any more questions?" He looks around the wardroom. Officers shake their heads.

Individuals now stand to leave for places of duty. Lieutenant Sutton, as he glances around the room, catches sight of the Royal Air Force liaison officer who has just delivered briefings. The air force officer has been placed in an unusual and awkward situation. In the event of a call to 'action stations', the flight lieutenant is probably the one man on board with no designated station. So where, wonders Sutton , will the RAF man go? What should he do? Perhaps he will join other aircrew in the hangar deck; maybe he'll make for the 'goofers' gallery' on the carrier's island; he may even elect to retire to his cabin.

Lieutenant Sutton cannot know that the flight lieutenant's invidious position will cause him embarrassment tomorrow and that as a result – perhaps in the absence of other ideas – he will decide to head for the wardroom. In spite of the commander's recent warning, Lieutenant

Sutton and others cannot predict how the imminence and the ferocity of Luftwaffe activity will exceed all expectations. He cannot realise the extent of tomorrow's devastation, how the loss of life will include the Royal Air Force man's cruel demise by decapitation. And he cannot anticipate how all of this will occur in less than twenty-four hours from now.

2

Heroic Heritage

A few officers remain in earnest conversation as others disperse from the wardroom after the briefing. Lieutenant Sutton decides to join aircrew colleagues who make for the carrier's hangar deck. As he enters the after end of the hangar, situated directly above the wardroom, he observes the numbers of Swordfish and Fulmar aircraft stacked together tightly, wings folded to allow maximum use of the available space. The machines are serviced by qualified maintainers who hasten around the area, individuals urgent in their efforts to carry out necessary procedures. He notes how the machines' camouflaged paint-work seems to emphasise their business-like air, the no-nonsense aura of the fighting unit.

He deliberates on the capabilities of HMS *Illustrious* with her motto *Vox Non Incerta* (No Uncertain Sound) and how her presence in the Mediterranean has transformed the region's balance of power since her arrival last summer. He gazes at the complexities of technical arrangement within the hangar, the intricate pipe-work threaded along bulkheads, the brightly coloured markings to signify fuel points, connections for electric power, oil, water, high pressure air, all the paraphernalia needed to manage the carrier's core purpose.

As he glances up at the deck-head, he sees how the area's headroom of just sixteen feet is packed with a multiplicity of spare parts: aircraft engines; airscrews; wheels; tyres; long-range fuel tanks. Above him, too, metal fire-screen curtains are rolled and stowed, ready to be dropped to form three separate compartments in the event of emergency. These fire-screens have demonstrated their worth in past incidents but, naturally, no one can appreciate just now how they will exacerbate tomorrow's impending disaster. The deck-head has other in-built safety features: across the whole expanse and at the turn of a switch, sprinklers a few inches apart have been designed to spray jets of salt water.

The lieutenant, impressed by the bustle of activity around him, watches the maintainers at work. Their reputation, as with other crew members on HMS *Illustrious*, is one of battle-hardened efficiency, duly respected by all in the Mediterranean Fleet. The *Illustrious*'s crewmen are renowned for their stern loyalty and the ship's very presence could reassure her allies, while generating fear within enemy ranks. He reflects on the effectiveness of the pipe-smoking ship's captain, Captain Dennis Boyd. The captain's steady influence would inspire his crew to tackle challenges and dangers sometimes beyond the call of duty. The men's daily routines are managed in spite of the lack of comforts on board, especially for the lower ranks who live in cramped mess decks beneath the waterline and who have to sling hammocks at night. The stuffy atmosphere below decks and the airless conditions ensure that few, no matter how fatigued, could enjoy the luxury of a good night's rest.

A stoker would record his impressions thus:

'Shipboard living conditions for ratings under the rank of petty officer were rough and ready to put it mildly. The lower stoker's mess deck was below the waterline and therefore had no portholes. The upper mess deck was above and portholes could be opened for fresh air during the day. At night, however, it was another story when we had to darken ship and all scuttles and dead-lights had to be closed. For air circulation we had only our forced air ventilation through small louvres on the head ducts. This was wartime and in the hot climate of the Med, or the tropics of the Red Sea, a crowded mess deck was stifling.

'We all needed to sleep somehow so we just sweated it out until it was time to go on watch. The navy had strict standards of hygiene and cleanliness. Messes had to be cleaned and scrubbed out every morning and everything put away. Hammocks had to be properly lashed up and stowed and no gear was to be left lying around. After meals, dishes and utensils had to be cleaned and tidied away. Before night rounds, mess decks were scrubbed and tidied up by 2100 when the duty officer and duty petty officer would do the night inspections.'

The lieutenant ponders the commander's recent briefing, how the revelation of harsh facts had intensified the ominous mood within the wardroom. "The Regia Aeronautica will be on the prowl," the commander had said, "and we can expect Luftwaffe intervention quite soon." However, in spite of his sense of unease, he retains confidence in his ship and in the ability of the men he now observes. Luftwaffe or not, his attitude is positive when he considers the *Illustrious*'s powerful capabilities, and her crew's talents at maximising their ship's potential.

After all this is the pride of the Illustrious class of ships, that new and radical category of carrier developed just a few years ago, in the mid-1930s. He recalls how the *Illustrious*, the *Victorious*, and the *Formidable* were the initial batch of a total of six aircraft carriers in the Illustrious class, all of which incorporated technical innovation to combat the toughest of foes. The carriers were fitted with the latest in anti-aircraft weaponry which included dozens of two-pound multiple pom-poms (Chicago pianos) and sixteen dual-purpose 4.5-inch guns. Flight-deck armour several inches thick provided physical protection, and the ingenious, new-fangled radar system gave advance warning of air attack.

The first in the class to be built, HMS *Illustrious* herself, gestated at about the time the lieutenant decided to volunteer for the Fleet Air Arm. The Admiralty's order for the ship was placed almost exactly four years ago, on 13 January 1937. The firm of Vickers-Armstrong, the carrier's constructors whose yard was at Barrow-in-Furness, allocated the yard number 732 to their new and esteemed assignment. The evolving carrier – over 753 feet long with a beam of just under ninety-six feet, a draft of some twenty-four feet – would become the fourth Royal Naval ship destined to bear the *Illustrious* name.

Vickers-Armstrong staff worked long hours on their prestigious project. Naval architects produced around 2,500 plans for the ship's bulk, with further drawings for her machinery. The ship's keel was laid within a matter of months and work forged ahead at a rapid pace. While welders and fitters fashioned her superstructure plate by plate, men with cranes lowered her boilers, swung on board heavy gear, and transferred specialist equipment. Before long, an advance guard of Royal Naval personnel arrived to monitor the ship as she evolved from a metal ant-heap that swarmed with dockyard workers. Co-operation was good and the builders, unfamiliar with the complexities of carrier construction, demonstrated admirable commitment as the months went by.

When the rust-coloured carcass on the Vickers-Armstrong's slip-way gradually assumed the form of a carrier's hull, more key officers and senior ratings were sent by the Royal Navy to advise on operational and other requirements. Swift progress continued, and within just two years of her laying down the ship was ready to be launched. On 5th April 1939, with the country a matter of months away from war, men and women at the Vickers-Armstrong yard heard the clatter of tangled chains unfold, squinted their eyes in the dusty, rust-filled air, marvelled at the achievements of dockyard and other personnel, clapped their hands and cheered as they saw the new carrier glide gracefully into the waters of Morecambe Bay.

Another year followed before the ship was ready for sea trials; the tasks during that period were varied and legion. The armoured flight-deck, prefabricated away from Barrow, had to be despatched in sections for assembly at the yard. Two large holes were carved for the aircraft lifts fore and aft. The carrier's island was constructed to accommodate the bridge and flying control, and the single large funnel. Gear was added: constituent machinery; ammunition hoists; storage tanks for aviation fuel; pipe-work to convey the fuel; more pipe-work for fire-fighting purposes. Specialist engineers installed radio panels, compasses, and radar gadgetry. Vickers-Armstrong electricians fixed up light and power circuits, telephone systems, fire-control units, air conditioning fans; shipwrights stowed cables and anchors; carpenters fitted-out chart-houses, messes, wardroom, medical centre, operations rooms, cabins while plumbers installed basins, showers, and waste-pipes.

Fresh water was a particular problem on the new carrier. The ship had four evaporators, two port and two starboard, with priority given to the carrier's three giant boilers. With the navy's insistence on high standards of personal hygiene, at times crewmen would be obliged to use salt water to wash and shave. Showers were available, although junior ratings tended to wash by throwing buckets of water over themselves. The distilled water produced by the evaporators was salt free but tasteless.

This perhaps accounted for the continued tradition on HMS *Illustrious* of the old navy custom of grog, introduced in 1740 by Admiral Edward Vernon, a man who habitually wore a waterproof cloak made of grogram fabric and who had earned, therefore, the nickname 'Old Grogram'. Some men seemed especially keen to purge the unpleasant tastelessness of the distilled water. Vernon's original mixture, one part rum to four parts water with the addition, to thwart scurvy, of lemon juice and brown sugar, had evolved over 200 years. Nowadays the new, improved (?) formula incorporated a mix of one-third rum to two-thirds water. The lieutenant remembers the anecdotes about crewmen's attempts to reserve personal grog rations with hand-written signs: 'I've spat in it.' (The signs, however, were prone to unofficial postscripts: 'so have I.') Of course, such notes should be unnecessary in an age where the need for trust is urged upon crew members. The daily grog ration (for non-commissioned ranks only) would be made available to *Illustrious* crewmen at 1100 hours, although most personnel tended to wait until they came off watch.

The lieutenant recalls how a new 'general messing' system of catering had been devised for the *Illustrious*'s crew. Food would be prepared centrally before collection by the cook of the day from each mess. Although the food was plain, most men understood that they fared, in all probability, better than their families back at home. The lieutenant is mindful, too, how current constraints could seem minor compared to those of forebears. Maybe present-day grumbles would ease, he thinks, if men reflected on the era when sailors were forced to consume rancid butter, bread infested with weevils, stale biscuits crumbled with age, beef salted almost beyond the point of edibility, meat with more fat and gristle than flesh. When even those meagre rations became short in supply, the sailors were obliged to catch fish, and even rats…

"Alfie, old fellow!" at the sound of his nickname, the lieutenant turns to glance behind. He sees a member of aircrew, a fellow observer, hasten up. "Alfie – are you programmed to fly this afternoon?"

"The doctor's declared me unfit to fly for the next couple of days."

"What have you been up to?"

"I've picked up an ear infection, I'm afraid."

The observer nods and asks: "What did you make of the commander's briefing?"

"As he pointed out," says Lieutenant Sutton, with a shrug, "it was just a matter of time before Jerry decided to join in the fray."

"I suppose Jerry's still sore as hell about Taranto," says the colleague. He gazes at the rows of aircraft stowed in the hangar, the urgent activity of the maintainers. "Though I don't understand why the admiral has to take us so close to Malta. Why can't we operate away from the rest of the fleet?"

"The admiral says our presence gives his other ships a boost."

"I could suggest other ways to give his ships a boost."

"Such as?"

"Something radical!" The observer chuckles. "How about importing a few women on board ship?"

"Women on board?"

"You never know your luck," he says with a wink.

"Some hope!"

"It happened in Nelson's day," says the observer. "But I must get a move on. I'm scheduled to fly and we'll be launching soon."

"Good luck." Lieutenant Sutton nods farewell as his colleague hastens across the hangar, weaving his way between the rows of Swordfish and Fulmar aircraft. He frowns. Nelson's day? Women on board ship? The complications, the implications…although, he ruminates, it was true that women *were* known to have been on board ships during the Battle of Trafalgar. The women, whose presence on board was not recognised officially, offered their services as powder monkeys, first aid attendants, and surgeons' assistants. It was known how, in frenetic and frightful scenes, surgeons would yell instructions to these women and to other helpers – 'loblolly' lads – as well as to the ship's purser and the padre summonsed to act as assistant surgeons. Personnel must have anticipated with dread the journey down ladders to reach the orlop deck below the waterline where lanterns and candles were set up to direct light onto the operating table. These, however, must have done little to dispel the surrounding gloom, the stifling and claustrophobic atmosphere, or the sense of entry into the Hall of Hades.

Of course, thinks Lieutenant Sutton, such conditions have been confined to the past. Today's seafarers can take comfort in the knowledge that modern ships are equipped with efficient and humane sickbays manned by well-qualified personnel. The Royal Navy's current insistence on regular rehearsal of first aid and other emergency drills may be taken to the point of tedium, nonetheless the drills helped to establish men's confidence in their own capabilities, and those of their ship.

A positive attitude was inculcated in the crew of HMS *Illustrious* at an early stage, the men's pride in their ship stemming from the first days when, in the spring of last year, the *Illustrious*'s boarding procedures commenced. The lieutenant and other aircrew had joined the ship some weeks later, but he had heard how the workers at Vickers-Armstrong were greatly impressed on Tuesday, 16th April 1940, when they witnessed the arrival of the 101 disciplines needed to form a carrier's crew: seamen; stokers; stewards; signal-men; storekeepers; sick-berth attendants; clerks; cooks; coders; marines; gunners…a population equivalent to that of a small town.

As crew members converged on the Vickers-Armstrong yard, as men climbed the ship's boarding ramps and walked her flight-deck, numbers gradually swelled towards the planned complement of some 1,400 personnel. The carrier soon teemed with life and activity. Officers and men were anxious to inspect their next place of duty, to view for themselves the new carrier that had dominated thoughts, dreams, and to evaluate the ship whose destiny would dictate their own.

Crewmen familiarised themselves with the arrangement of mess decks, passageways, ladders, and the general layout. Men inspected their workplaces where all would be expected to operate effectively, be praised or admonished, encouraged or censured, befriended or disliked. Experienced seamen analysed the action station's routes when alarms shrieked and when men would leap from mess bench or hammock to snatch protective gear and sea boots before hastening to points of duty. Old hands met up with shipmates from past commissions; younger men appeared apprehensive. Everyone had to accept cheerfully their changed circumstance and the immediate future where individuals would live, serve their country, and possibly die in the process.

A week or so after the commencement of her boarding procedures, the *Illustrious* first went to sea. With a destroyer escort, the carrier began constructor's trials as she steamed south from Barrow towards Liverpool. The essential procedures, before a ship could be declared fully functional, were carried out: the carrier's compasses were swung; her echo sounder proved; her pitometer log calibrated; the telegraphs to her three engine rooms tested; her steering gear evaluated. The open waters of the Irish Sea proved ideal before the ship dry-docked in Liverpool for a short period. Here, bilge keels were fitted and three permanent bronze screws were installed to replace the temporary cast-iron ones.

The bulk of the carrier's ammunition was received at Liverpool, and shortly after departure from there the ship's gunners had their first opportunity to test-fire her guns. By then, however, the demands of the Norwegian campaign, the desperate situation in France, and the looming evacuation of the British Army at Dunkirk, had forced the Admiralty to issue orders for the carrier's sea trials to be reduced to the minimum. HMS *Illustrious* was commissioned officially on 25th May 1940, just one month after her initial sea trials. A few weeks later, her three squadrons arrived in time for the ship's departure to the calmer waters of Bermuda where she would work-up to operational standards.

Lieutenant Sutton looks up sharply. He stares towards a sudden disturbance at one end of the hangar. A maintainer has dropped some equipment, now his curses are interspersed with those of the supervising petty officer. There is little wonder, he thinks, that the ratings become overwrought; perhaps these men are due for a break soon. In terms of naval accommodation, HMS *Illustrious* shows progress in one way at least: the provision of a ratings' recreation room where a civilian NAAFI manager serves soft drinks. The lieutenant sees the supervising petty officer speak to his rating; both men then appear to calm down and the hangar's atmosphere returns to what passes for normality.

As the lieutenant continues to watch the activities around him, he ponders the heroic naval heritage which has led to the modern HMS *Illustrious*, her development from the crude seventy-four-gun frigate that first bore the *Illustrious* name at the time of Nelson. Launched at Bucklers Hard, Hampshire, in 1789, the first HMS *Illustrious* saw action against enemy warships and was instrumental in the capture of two others. He remains convinced that the present-day ship with her up-to-date techniques, her latest in technical ingenuity, will triumph against the Luftwaffe and the Regia Aeronautica. Admiral Cunningham's decision to keep the carrier in close company with other ships in convoy is less than ideal but understandable, and the lieutenant's faith in the carrier and her capabilities remains staunch.

He has no inkling at present, of course, of the extent of tomorrow's ordeals, how the anguish endured by forebears will prove no less severe for the modern sailor, or how the ghosts of Nelson's heroes will rise as if to warn their scions that the spirit of *Vox Non Incerta* will be tested more soundly and more certainly than ever can be imagined just now.

3

Conversation with a Marine

When he exits the hangar deck, Lieutenant Sutton spots the approach of his Royal Marine servant, Marine Tregaskis. "Everything's in order in your cabin, sir," says the marine by way of conversation as both men come to a halt.

"Thanks, Tregaskis. I'm just heading there now."

"Are you fit to fly yet, sir?"

"Not for day or two."

"Sorry to hear you're unwell, sir." The lieutenant nods appreciatively. He contemplates with gratitude the naval regulation – seen by some as from a bygone era – that allows officers of sufficient seniority to the entitlement, even in wartime, of a marine servant. These men, charged with bodyguard duties and, additionally, with attending to an officer's personal kit, are renowned for fierce loyalty towards their officers. However, other marine roles on board ship – wardroom attendants, members of the marine band, manning of anti-aircraft and other guns – would take precedence over marine servant tasks.

"I've heard rumours about a full flying programme ahead, sir," says Marine Tregaskis, a future fleet master-at-arms.

"The Germans have decided, it seems, to rally round their Italian friends. No doubt we'll hear action stations piped before long."

"Will you go to the hangar deck as normal when we hear action stations piped?"

"The commander's short-handed on the bridge so he's asked me to help out there. We're due to rendezvous with a convoy from Gibraltar tomorrow morning and I'm sure life will become hectic as we near the Pantelleria Straits and Malta."

"Things look bad in Malta these days."

The lieutenant shrugs. "The resilience of the Maltese goes back a long way."

"I'm sure, sir, that they're not keen on the idea of invasion by Mussolini."

"Did you hear about Admiral Cunningham's recent visit to Malta? Locals turned out in large numbers to cheer him. Malta's dockyard facilities are as vital to his Mediterranean Fleet as the bases at Gibraltar and Alexandria."

"Talking of Alex, sir," says Marine Tregaskis, "did you receive some suitable BOLTOP when we were in port?"

"BOLTOP?"

The marine grins. "The lads get these coded messages in letters from girlfriends. BOLTOP means: 'Better On The Lips Than On Paper.'"

"So true."

"Then there's HOLLAND – 'Hope Our Love Lasts And Never Dies'."

"Any others?"

"There's ITALY, of course: 'I'm Thinking About Loving You.'"

"What about MALTA?"

"I don't believe so, sir. We could always make one up."

"How about: 'Mussolini's Arrogance Leaves Tarts Appalled?'"

"Sounds okay, sir," says Marine Tregaskis doubtfully. "I'll suggest it to the lads, like. We could even tell it..." he laughs and raises his eyes heavenwards, "to poor old Solomon Grundy – born on Monday, christened on Tuesday."

"What about Wednesday?"

"Married on Wednesday, took ill on Thursday. Worse on Friday, died on Saturday. Buried on Sunday, that was the end of Solomon Grundy."

"What day of the week is this, Tregaskis?"

"Thursday I believe, sir, though time seems a bit unreal just now."

"Tomorrow's Friday, then. The prospects don't look encouraging."

"We shouldn't worry about it, sir. We'll concentrate on cheerful thoughts; keep our spirits up, like. Although with these reports in the newspapers about the bombing of London, things don't look good on the home front at present. Even St Paul's Cathedral was hit."

"Hitler wanted revenge after the Battle of Britain and now his bombers time their raids to coincide with tidal low-water on the River Thames. The firemen struggle to find enough water."

"At least, sir," says the marine, "we've managed to put a stop to this invasion business. As Churchill pointed out recently: 'We're still waiting for the long-promised invasion. So are the fishes.'" The men chuckle at this.

"Hitler must have forgotten the lessons of history."

"He was surely taken aback by our resilience during the Battle of Britain."

"Fighter Command did incredibly well despite the shortage of pilots. However, the supply of aircraft appeared to keep going even though normally we never have enough."

"Aircraft always seem to be in short supply, sir."

"Blame our leaders. Remind them about our Stringbags, rugged machines they may be, but they can't go on forever."

"No disrespect, sir, but they *do* look a bit antiquated, like some relic from the last war."

"It's all part of the plan, Tregaskis," says the lieutenant, grinning. "We've got to fool Jerry somehow or other."

"Fair point, sir. And let's face it, the Stringbags did an amazing job at the Taranto raid. Which reminds me...what do you make of the rumpus stirred up about the allocation of awards after Taranto? The lads were disgusted, the notices of awards were torn down from boards."

"We suffered remarkably few casualties at Taranto, but whether that should influence the allocation of awards..." the lieutenant shrugs. "It's to do with the fog of war, I suppose. The general confusion was hardly helped by initial press reports that the attack had been carried out by the Royal Air Force."

"As always, the Fleet Air Arm is kept in the shade."

"The truth," says the lieutenant, "comes out in time. Inter-service rivalries are..."

"The same as in the last war, sir?"

"Probably. But what are your duties just now, Tregaskis? Are you headed for the wardroom?"

"Yes, sir. I've got things to sort out there, including the display of this evening's menus."

"Are we to be offered the privilege of choice?"

"I doubt that, though there are rumours that the cooks intend to concoct a special 'Woolton Pie'." The marine lowers his voice to one of hushed respect. "Root vegetables, cauliflower, onions, parsley, and oatmeal. That little lot will be topped with mashed potatoes and grated cheese. We may have to do without the cauliflower and the parsley, though."

"And the cheese?"

"That too."

"I'll look forward to supper, then."

"There should be enough tea to drink."

"Ah, tea! How famous is our tea."

"Sir?"

"If all else fails, Tregaskis, we can look forward to drinking tea."

"Indeed, sir, unless we're rationed."

"Tea rationing? Not on board ship, anyway. As for the food..."

Marine Tregaskis snorts derisively. "We do our best," he says, "against all odds. It's become a common topic with the lads. In their letters from home they read the moans of wives and girlfriends; the boring and expensive food, how everyone is fed up with vegetable pie, spam, boiled potatoes. As for getting hold of an egg, like..."

"You have to be a fighter pilot to qualify for an egg." The lieutenant checks his watch. "I should get a move on now, Tregaskis. The commander's given me a few tasks and I've got some reports to write up. But it's been good to have a chat..."

"Yes, sir, and I must proceed with my wardroom duties."

"Good luck with those."

"Thanks, sir." The marine grins as the two men part and as the lieutenant resumes the journey towards his cabin. While he reflects on his high regard for Marine Tregaskis, he remembers the marine's assistance last year on a crowded troop train when the newly-married Lieutenant and Mrs Sutton had moved from their first home near the airfield at Ford. Marine Tregaskis had taken charge of the couple's luggage and personal kit, had acted as bodyguard, companion, friend. The lieutenant is conscious of his good fortune, no doubt, but he cannot predict how his marine servant's presence is about to become of life-saving significance.

4

Just Dreams?

The single cabin allocated to Lieutenant Sutton is small (about six square feet), but appreciated by him nonetheless. The cramped accommodation on board HMS *Illustrious* means that officers with a lesser seniority on the all-important naval list may have to share two or more to a cabin. As he pushes open his cabin door, he knows that the room, despite its miniscule size in relation to the aircraft carrier's overall bulk, still represents valued space, a small spot in the ocean where he can have some privacy. He sympathises with the carrier's lower ranked crew members who lack any such refuge.

He glances at the family photos on a bulkhead in his cabin. One of the photos, taken last year on 24th January 1940, is of his wedding at Buckfast Abbey in Devonshire. He had requested leave for the day's first anniversary but now, with just weeks before the due date, the prospect seems remote.

He gazes at the pictures of groups and individuals who, at the wedding photographer's behest, stand shivering on the snow-covered steps. He thinks about the curious circumstances, some two-and-a-half years before, which led to his meeting his future wife. He was second lieutenant on the destroyer HMS *Basilisk* at the time.

On the completion of patrol duties along the northern coast of Spain during the Spanish Civil War, the ship would reposition at Saint-Jean-de-Luz in order to prepare for her next period of patrol. It was on one such harbour-bound occasion that he was asked (told) by the ship's captain to attend a cocktail party hosted by the British ambassador, Sir Henry Chilton. The ambassador, then in Hendaye in southern France in order to avoid the dangers of the civil war, had invited the Royal Navy to send two officers to his cocktail party. Lieutenant Sutton and a colleague from HMS *Basilisk*, although less than enthusiastic, were selected. The captain had pointed out that this was a necessary part of naval commitment.

However, on the day of the cocktail party, Lieutenant Sutton, while in conversation with an elderly lady, had caught sight of an attractive young woman. Suddenly he felt rather more enthusiastic about the event. The girl had disappeared in the crowded room but eventually he spotted her again. He then decided to ask the elderly lady to arrange an introduction but could the meeting, perhaps, be arranged for another, less formal, occasion? This lady, if somewhat taken aback, nonetheless agreed to the suggestion and a dinner party was planned for a few days later.

The young woman turned out to be Miss Mary Margaret Cazeaux de Grange (known as Peggy), a member of an aristocratic family forced out of Spain by the troubles. When the young couple's friendship blossomed into romance, they met as often as possible although they did not become formally engaged. Shortly after the outbreak of war with Germany, he had written to Miss Cazeaux to ask for her hand in marriage.

The wedding arrangements had been the responsibility of his mother alone, as she, poor woman, had to cope without the support of her husband. His mother, widowed in 1916 when his father was killed in the Battle of the Somme, had brought up her two young sons on her own. In the photographs, he sees the tension on her face, the similar anxiety of the bride's mother, expressions that contrasted with the look of joy on the face of the bride herself, by then Mrs Peggy Sutton. He ponders other faces, including those conspicuous by their absence. The bride's father was not present because of illness and this seemed, somehow, to underline the sense of loss caused by the absence of the groom's own father. Just four years old at the time of his father's death, Lieutenant Sutton has no memories of him; to learn of his father he has had to rely on old photographs and brief conversations with his mother.

How he wishes he could speak to his father. There are so many things they could discuss together. What, for example, were his father's personal experiences leading up to the fateful morning of 1st July 1916, the day when vast numbers of Allied infantrymen had begun assaults in a remote part of France dominated by the River Somme? General Haig, who had ordered artillery bombardments a week before the infantry assaults, had stated his objectives. But had the lieutenant's father and his fellow soldiers been briefed properly, on the bigger picture, the plan to capture German defences along the Thiepval-Pozières heights before the troops pressed on to Bapaume, or were the men kept in ignorance?

The initial attacks that day began at 0730, with subsequent waves ordered 'over the top' throughout the morning. What, speculates Sutton, was the prevalent atmosphere within his father's unit and how did this alter as the day progressed? Perhaps they were confident at first, but did feelings of fury finally grip the British infantrymen when they began to realise the full folly of their orders, the awesome destruction caused by German machine-gun fire? Maybe, at first, the warm July sunshine had lulled minds into states of unreality. Eventually, though, this must have changed. What agitation was stirred by the image of close colleagues who, as they were shot, fell on top of an accumulated mass of young men, those already wounded, dying or dead? What mental machinations were needed to cope with the sights, the sounds, the smells – the bloodied carpet of khaki that writhed and heaved and moaned on that foul French soil?

How did men react to the realisation that within a matter of hours (perhaps less), over 20,000 British soldiers had been killed, twice that number wounded? The event had turned into the biggest fiasco in military history. No amount of explanation, no volume of apologetic howling, could absolve its authors or the murderous incompetence of the army hierarchy at large, that of General Haig and General Rawlinson in particular. Why were these two men not held to account at court martial? The generals' sublime belief that their artillery barrage would allow the infantrymen safely to 'stroll over the fields' was summed up by a German soldier, Karl Blenk:

'When the English started to advance we were very worried; they looked as though they would definitely over-run our trenches. But we were surprised to see them walking, we had never seen that before. Everywhere I looked I could see English soldiers. The officers were in front. I noticed one of them coming forth slowly as he carried a walking stick. When we opened fire we just had to load and reload. They went down in their hundreds. You didn't even have to aim, just fire into them. If only they had run, they would have overwhelmed us.'

So what, wonders Lieutenant Sutton, were his father's feelings before 'going over the top?' He had heard accounts of men's agonies of anticipation, the dreadful tick of the minutes and seconds before the whistle was blown. The staunch British Tommy must have waited for the countdown as if anticipating the hangman's noose; even experienced veterans were not quite sure how they would react next time. Some men shook like leaves; some became numb with apprehension. Soldiers were as fearful of showing cowardice in front of friends as they were of being struck by an enemy bullet.

Married personnel attempted to scribble notes to their wives, but would the notes be passed on and what should be said? The trench environment, hardly conducive to elaborate farewell notes, was full of uncertainties. As they waited with fixed bayonets, tin helmets on heads, some men would try to crack jokes, some would remain silent, and most wondered if the cigarette they smoked would be their last. Perhaps like others his father had a sense of premonition that he would not survive. Going 'over the top' was a collective act but every man still had a terrible and haunting awareness of personal vulnerability. When the whistle was blown, and soldiers began to launch themselves into no man's land, survivors would recount how, once they had to go, they had a personal plan of action in their minds. Some believed the best way was to shoot straight up the ladder as fast as possible, while others preferred to hold back momentarily.

The lieutenant shakes his head slowly, and reflects on the act of madness that triggered the world conflict, the deed of student nationalist Gavrilo Princip who assassinated Archduke Franz Ferdinand, heir to the Austro-Hungarian empire, and his wife at Sarajevo on 28th June 1914. Of course, most people expected such an act to precipitate war, but most thought the war would be short-lived. A month or so later when Britain, on 4th August 1914, became the only power to declare war on Germany rather than the other way around, and the chain reaction of war declarations had become unstoppable and armies had begun to congregate, most still thought that the war would be over by Christmas.

Both sides were equally convinced that their cause was right, that God marched with them (the belt buckles of German soldiers carried the words '*Got mit uns*' – God with us); both sides were equally appalled, no doubt, when leaders spoke about the possibility of war beyond Christmas. In Britain, inspired by the announcement of the war minister, Earl Kitchener, that the war could last as long as three or four years, that the country would need to raise an army of 'many millions', a wave of patriotic enthusiasm persuaded men to volunteer.

When those years had evaporated, and Kitchener himself had drowned after the ship that was carrying him to Russia had struck a mine, news of that event had reached German trenches and a German *feldgrau* had started to bang his mess tin in a gesture of derision – a call that spread from man to man, trench to trench, area to area, mile after mile until the entire 450-mile network had erupted into an underground clatter of contempt – by then the realities of the Great War had brought about new attitudes.

Wilfrid Owen in his *Dulce et Decorum Est* (the title taken from a line in Horace's 'How sweet and noble it is to die for one's country') would describe the scene as a group of soldiers abandoned the trenches for a rest centre at the rear.

> *Bent double, like old beggars under sacks,*
> *Knock-kneed, coughing like hags, we cursed through sludge,*
> *Till on the haunting flares we turned our backs*

JUST DREAMS?

And towards our distant rest began to trudge.
Men marched asleep. Many had lost their boots
But limped on, blood-shod. All went lame; all blind;
Drunk with fatigue; deaf even to the hoots
Of tired, outstripped Five-Nines that dropped behind.

What shock of excess, wonders the lieutenant, what fatigue must be endured in order to paralyse a man's sense of vigilance against the perils of German 'Five-Nine' artillery shells falling close by? Perhaps something even worse, he thinks, something to arouse an even deeper terror, an even greater sense of abhorrence at the prospect of another from the Great War's great arsenal of depravity...

Gas! Gas! Quick boys! – An ecstasy of fumbling,
Fitting the clumsy helmets just in time;
But someone was still yelling out and stumbling,
And flound'ring like a man on fire or lime...
Dim, through the misty panes and thick green light,
As under a green sea, I saw him drowning.

In all my dreams, before my helpless sight,
He plunges at me, guttering, choking, drowning.

If in some smothering dreams you too could pace
Behind the wagon that we flung him in,
And watch the white eyes writhing in his face,
His hanging face, like a devil's sick of sin;
If you could hear, at every jolt, the blood
Come gargling from the froth-corrupted lungs,
Obscene as cancer, bitter as the cud
Of vile, incurable sores on innocent tongues –
My friend, you would not tell me with such high zest.

To children ardent for some desperate glory,
The old Lie: Dulce et Decorum est
Pro patria mori.

The lieutenant glances out of his cabin porthole. He stares at the slate grey sea whipped darker in places by the wind, at the steady swell of the mid-winter waters of the Mediterranean. Words still run through his mind; he continues to agonise about his late father's fate. Did he suffer for long? Perhaps there were final dreams of deliverance, the wider windows of calm, congenial visions; the picture of back home, his wife, their two young sons. The older of the two, Alan, would turn to look back, reach out, smile. There would be a room, cosily welcome, vases filled with flowers, their sweet scent distinctive; the crackle of a log fire in an open hearth; good food to be shared with those who cared. Through the room's window would be green fields – sharp and clear – and rolling hills. Music would fill the room, Puccini perhaps, one of his finest arias, Doretta's dream...

With a sigh, Lieutenant Sutton gazes again at the photographic images on the nearby bulkhead. If only his father had been present at the wedding, surely he would have been proud of his elder son. If only... he tries to picture his father's look of approval, the observation of a young man in naval lieutenant's uniform, naval sword clasped, one arm gripped by a bride, so beautiful. Yes, he would have been proud, even though pride, as revealed by Robert Browning, could expose tender complexity.

> *Pride? – when those eyes forestall the life behind*
> *The death I have to go through! – when I find,*
> *Now that I want thy help the most, all of thee!*
> *What did I fear? Thy love shall hold me fast*
> *Until the little minute's sleep is past*
> *And I wake saved. – And yet it will not be!*

Will not be? Could not be...perhaps, reflects the lieutenant, the abiding vexation of Hamlet had crept closer to the truth... 'To die, to sleep; to sleep, perchance to dream. Ay, there's the rub; for in that sleep of death what dreams may come...'

Dreams! Men spoke about the daily struggle of trench life, how this could seem dream-like. There were reports of soldiers wandering through no man's land, completely lost. What were the conditions on the morning of 1st July 1916? Perhaps, before 0730, there was a paradoxical start to the day, a natural world of grace and beauty, wild poppies hanging over parapets, the song of birds overhead, the stir of vivid butterflies. As men waited for the big push, as they snatched hasty breakfasts, perhaps there was talk of iron rations, hard tack biscuits, Maconochie stew – MM (the 'Maconochie Medal' for eating the stuff), JUO (Jam of Uncertain Origin). Perhaps there was nervous banter – talk of Jerries (Germans) and Jacks (military police), of puttees, gorblimeys (field service caps), hospital blues, trench foot, identity discs – the waterproof tags that bore a soldier's name, number, unit and religion. Of the two identity discs issued, one was coloured green and remained on the corpse as a means of identification in the event of reburial. The second disc, coloured red, was removed from the corpse as proof of death.

Perhaps the men chatted about another form of trench warfare: the battle against rats. As on board ships in Nelson's time, rats were abundant in the trenches of the Great War. Even in flooded conditions, the creatures would be present, their noses poking above the water as they swam through the trenches. The rats, described by soldiers as 'big as bloomin' cats', showed astonishing boldness and ingenuity as they sought out food. The creatures would gnaw their way through packs and kit bags, swiftly consuming the contents despite the best efforts of soldiers to protect precious supplies. At night, the rats' eyes would flash in the candlelight. As soon as the candles were extinguished, the rats would topple them in order to eat the candle-wax.

Soldiers sleeping in trenches and dugouts would try to ignore the rodents' omnipresence; men would throw blankets over themselves in efforts to sleep as the rats scampered across prone figures. If a blanket slipped from a slumbering soldier, the man might wake with a start as his gaping mouth felt the twitch of rodent whiskers, the slither of a rat's hind leg, or the malodour of the creature's urine.

The rats were not the sole cause of the soldiers' domestic discomfort. As Nelson's sailors suffered lice infestation, so did the soldiers in the trenches. Young infantrymen new to the line would be embarrassed to discover personal lice in shirts or underwear. Secrecy would be brief, though, because word soon got out that everybody was affected in a battle against a foe every bit as intractable as the enemy soldier. The parasites – generally whitish grey in colour – measured between three and four millimetres in length, and could live for around eight weeks. The lice would puncture a hole in the skin, then suck blood. Such a bite could lead an individual to uncontrollable itching and some men, driven mad by the itches, would scratch so much with dirty fingernails that blood poisoning would set in.

In attempts to keep the infestation under control, men would set fire to tapers of long waxy string, run the flame up and down clothing seams – even bare flesh – and watch with satisfaction as the abhorrent parasites fried. Men spoke about the Harrison's Pomade supplied by the army to kill lice, how this was found to be generally ineffective, and conversely how the lice eventually seemed to thrive on the stuff.

At least Nelson's sailors did not have to suffer the problem of mud. Soldiers in trenches, on the other hand, had to contend with trampled soil that became like liquid glue. Men became stuck fast; sometimes four or five soldiers were needed to dig out one individual. Even when a man's feet became exposed, rescuers found they could not break the suction until a shovel was placed under each foot forcibly to lever the man out of the ground.

In winter, it became common for soldiers to wade in trench water that was ankle, knee, even chest deep. Trench walls collapsed and occasionally the troops, both Allied and German, were forced onto parapets in full view of the enemy. When the men were relieved of front-line duty, they had to walk some seven or so miles to safety, usually at night. Soldiers were briefed to remain on duck-board tracks or risk getting stuck in the mud. Nevertheless, as the exhausted men carried rifles and heavy kit, some would slip off the boards and become trapped. The army issued orders that these personnel should be left; there had been too many instances of attempted rescue where the rescuers themselves had been pulled in. The abandoned soldiers often were stuck for hours – even days – by which stage individuals had begun to hallucinate to the point of insanity.

Lieutenant Sutton continues to stare out of his cabin porthole. He cannot avoid his sense of anger as he reflects on the brutal absurdity, the crazy fruitlessness, of the scenes imposed on the likes of his father. In the five months of abortive action that followed 1st July 1916, when generals on both sides pushed their men forward in fresh assaults that strived to out-rival each other as exercises in the futile, Allied and German armies fired 30,000,000 shells, suffered 1,000,000 casualties between them, and all of this in an area of just seven miles square.

As he meditates the hideous finality of the conditions endured and how the British Tommy of the Great War (the nickname derived from the hypothetical 'Thomas Atkins' used at the time of the Napoleonic Wars to show men how to fill out an army pay book) had been compelled to survive, more often than not, in environments deemed unsuitable even for animals, the lieutenant recalls the sentiments of Tom Kettle, a volunteer commander of the Royal Dublin Fusiliers, an Irish nationalist politician, essayist and poet. Kettle was mortally wounded on 9th September 1916, but shortly before his death, wrote these words:

'When the time comes to write down in every country a plain record of the war, with its wounds and weariness and flesh stabbing and bone pulverising and lunacies and rats and lice and maggots, and all the crawling festerment of battlefields, two landmarks in human progress will be revealed. The world will for the first time understand the nobility, beyond all phrase, of the soldiers, and it will understand also the foulness, beyond all phrase, of those who compel in war.'

A disturbance outside his cabin interrupts his thoughts. Looking back towards the door he sees a group of high-spirited young aircrew who laugh and banter while they pass by. As he reverts his gaze, he catches another glimpse of his mother's image. At the photographer's bid, she stands patiently on the steps of the abbey. He scrutinises her practical suit, and sensible sturdy shoes, her serious expression. What, he wonders, was she contemplating at that moment? Perhaps her thoughts were with her husband, how she craved his presence. The passage of twenty-five years since his death may have helped heal wounds but they will never disappear. He sees her composure – the British stiff upper lip – the firm bearing and determined gaze.

Perhaps, when she meditates the loss of her British Tommy and the wasted lives of so many millions, perhaps then the lure of a distant dream may induce an unwanted quiver of the stoical lip. Perhaps, though, in the sob of barren nights she just dreams for a just dream.

5

Wardroom Issues

That evening, as he hastens along a passageway from his cabin to the wardroom, Lieutenant Sutton is conscious of distant clatters from the hangar deck. He is aware of recent reconnaissance and bomber sorties flown by the Italian Regia Aeronautica, and he knows that Fulmar fighters from 806 Squadron are being made ready. Maintainers work rapidly to refuel and rearm the aircraft, and to prepare the machines for launch in anticipation of further enemy attacks. Meanwhile, as duty personnel carry out operational tasks, off-duty men attempt to carry on with a normal routine – at least, as ordinary a routine as circumstances permit.

While he proceeds along the passageway, he contemplates the anomalies created by the crewmen's system of on-duty/off-duty on a modern warship. Even when called to action stations, numbers of crew members will be stood down until needed to relieve workmates. Forebears, he recalls, experienced different constraints, including remarkable dress regulations, as ships' companies prepared *en masse* for action in wooden men o'war.

When Nelson's officers prepared for battle these men had to wear blue jackets with tails, white waistcoats and breeches. For headdress, the officers donned cocked hats worn with the two pointed ends over the shoulders. This was modified some years later when fashion demanded that the cocked hat should be worn with the points fore and aft. Officers were encouraged to put on clean clothes before battle, perhaps for luck, but in the knowledge, too, that dirty clothes could delay the healing of wounds.

While preparations for the Battle of Trafalgar were under way, Nelson's friend and rival, Admiral Collingwood, stopped a young officer, Lieutenant Clavell, to caution him: "You had better put on silk stockings as I have done, lieutenant," said the admiral. "If one should get shot in the leg, they would be so much more manageable for the surgeon." This was good advice: both men were injured in the battle, with the admiral seriously wounded in the leg when struck by a wood splinter.

The mode of dress for Nelson's lower deck men, however, was conspicuously different to that of their officers. The lieutenant has read about the times when most of the sailors, aware that the decks would become repressively hot (and progressively hotter) once the guns opened fire, preferred to go into battle naked from the waist up. Contrary to popular belief, Nelson's men – both officers and non-commissioned ranks – were not allowed to wear beards, although many of the sailors would shave just once a week when they smartened themselves up for Sunday church parade. The men liked to grow large sideburns, and these were permitted.

The distinction between officers and men was further emphasised by the type of footwear: as battle loomed, many of the sailors chose to discard their shoes so bare feet could seek a better grip on the sand-strewn decks. The lieutenant pictures the contrast of scenes before battle: the oil-spattered overalls of today's maintainers in the hangar; the burly sailors of Nelson's time who would adjust head bandages and handkerchiefs to soak up perspiration and to protect ears against surrounding clamour.

Intrigued by the notoriously paternalistic outlook of the Nelson era naval officers (foreign as well as British), Lieutenant Sutton sometimes wonders about such eccentric attitudes. With an extravagant disregard for personal safety, the officers would lead from the front as they ventured to win the respect of crewmen. The sailors had few qualms about seeking any available refuge from the lethal showers produced by enemy onslaught, but officers, as a point of honour, felt obliged to pace the decks proudly in fine clothing, apparently oblivious to the bullets and cannon balls that ricocheted around them.

This obsessive display of male virility was taken to extremes in the Battle of the Nile, seven years before Trafalgar, when the commander of the French Fleet, Admiral Brueys, had both of his legs shot away. Determined not to succumb to such limbless adversity (and ignoring the flow of blood from his head wound), the admiral insisted that he should be propped in an armchair on the quarter-deck. With all the appearance, so it seemed, of some hideous, manic rag doll, he continued to issue orders until he was hit by another cannonball that almost severed him in two. Still the admiral refused to relinquish his post. Remarkably, he resisted offers to take him below decks; unsurprisingly, he died within a short period.

On another French ship, Admiral Bruey's fellow officer, Admiral Dupetit-Thouars, was pointing with one arm when the limb was shot away. The admiral raised his other arm but this, too, was shot away. Rumours that the admiral then tried to raise one leg were probably speculative but the matter, in any case, became irrelevant when the leg was shot off. By now presumably devoid of ideas, the poor admiral sank to the deck. However, the comfort of an armchair was not for Dupetit-Thouars: he instructed his men to prop him against a bran barrel and to straighten his hat while he, too, persisted to give orders until the last.

Lieutenant Sutton adjusts the neatness of his bow tie and he rechecks his clean white shirt – carefully ironed and prepared by Marine Tregaskis – as he approaches the wardroom. As with other ships in the Royal Navy, the peacetime protocol of formal dinner in HMS *Illustrious*'s wardroom has been revised; officers now disregard the convention that all should enter the dining room together. Nevertheless, the officers still make efforts to meet for pre-dinner drinks where congenial conversations before the meal encourage a touch of civilisation in the carrier's otherwise harsh environment. Officers have been briefed that individuals may leave the anteroom for the dining area when they wish, as dictated by duty.

The full formalities of dress rules have been relaxed too, although officers are still required to wear a bow tie with a white shirt and naval uniform. As he nears the anteroom, the lieutenant hears the hum of conversation rise in volume. At the entrance, he pauses to peer inside the room. He notes officers' animated discussions and he sees, too, how the high standards of peacetime have been maintained in outward respects: items of mess silver have been put onto polished mahogany tables; generous armchairs, neatly laid-out newspapers and magazines, paintings of celebrated naval scenes…traditional embellishments have been placed carefully in order to enhance the wardroom's atmosphere of comfortable formality.

As he glances around the anteroom, the lieutenant observes the marine attendants on duty, although he cannot spot Marine Tregaskis; he assumes his personal marine servant has been detailed to act as attendant in the dining area. He starts to squeeze past groups of officers, then turns to look behind as his name is called out: "Alfie!" A fellow member of aircrew struggles to ease through the crush. "You still unfit to fly? Fit enough to manage a small pint, I trust?"

"Thanks old chap." The two progress slowly through the crowded anteroom while they aim for an area monopolised by 815 Squadron officers. They begin to pick up the drift of their colleagues' conversation:

"…the White Cliffs of Dover have been used as air raid shelters."

"The White Cliffs have witnessed some black scenes," says Lieutenant Sutton.

"Good evening," says a sub-lieutenant, glancing respectfully at the senior lieutenant. "Black scenes maybe, but I've heard that unusual things have been going on there recently."

"Oh?"

"Apparently, builders have constructed a form of central hall within the tunnels of the White Cliffs. Long galleries radiate outwards with rows of three-tier sleeping bunks to accommodate 2,000 people or more."

"2,000?"

"Yes."

"The image of the White Cliffs," says another officer, "must have raised a few..." he pauses to gulp at his drink. A lull in conversation is punctuated by helpful suggestions from colleagues:

"Eyebrows?"

"Travel expenses?"

"Kilt socks?"

"No!" guffaws the sub-lieutenant. He thumps down his beer mug. "I meant people's spirits. Think of the evacuation of the army from Dunkirk last year."

"The small ships made an awesome sight from the air," says a pilot. "Our squadron Swordfish were tasked to attack German torpedo boats – E-boats – before the enemy could interfere with the small ships. From above, the parallel lines of little ships looked like a series of stepping-stones packed tightly together."

"I was there too," says another pilot. "The assortment of craft was extraordinary...fishing vessels, oyster smacks, lifeboats, a Thames fireboat, even Thames barges under full sail. We had a bird's-eye view of history in the making. Never before, so they say, has such an armada put to sea spontaneously and without proper instructions or sailing orders of any kind. The spectacle was quite humbling, especially when viewed from an aircraft. The homeward-bound ships made up the centre columns, protected on their flanks by the Dunkirk-bound columns. Guarding the small ships were destroyers, mine-sweepers, any available naval ship flying the white ensign, and all crammed full with soldiers on the homeward run."

"There's a magazine article over there," a squadron observer nods towards a wardroom table, "about a coxswain on one of the lifeboat crews sent across from Kent. In order to save fuel, his lifeboat was towed across the Channel and when, at around midnight, they reached the vicinity of Dunkirk, he said there was an overwhelming stench of fire and smoke from infernos in the town and dock areas. The sea front was thick with smoke so the crew had to grope their way through sunken craft and hazardous flotsam. German shells burst overhead and in the fractured darkness the crew could make out Allied troops attempting to dig out small craft that had been beached. The water's edge was marked by mounds of debris, roaming cattle, even the charred remains of a pleasure steamer."

"The situation led to harsh inter-service accusations. The soldiers were bitter about the air force, remember?"

"That's crabs for you," an officer rolls his eyes heavenwards.

"Matters were not straightforward," says one of the pilots. "The aircraft operated out of the army's sight."

"Churchill said something about a victory inside the deliverance...that this was gained by the air force, that the soldiers coming back had not seen the RAF at work and that they should not underrate its achievements."

"I witnessed at first hand the activities of a squadron of Defiants," says a pilot. "The RAF fellows launched themselves remorselessly against formations of German bombers escorted by Me 109s and Me 110s. I tried to work out the numbers in the German formations but there were too many, it was impossible to count. Later that evening, I heard that the Defiants had shot down eighteen bombers in the morning, and twenty-one in the afternoon. When you consider this was the work of just one squadron..."

"The Dunkirk episode had unexpected repercussions," says an officer. "It was a military disaster and yet, in a curious way, it brought the nation together."

Lieutenant Sutton looks behind him at the sound of laughter from a nearby group. As he glances around, he is struck by the youthful appearance of many in the room, a sign, he reflects, of the navy's rapid expansion to meet the demands of the war. He catches sight of a sub-lieutenant in so-called 'Wavy Navy' uniform (The Royal Naval Volunteer Reserve), an unusual type, he thinks, to be posted to an aircraft carrier, a class of ship normally crewed by experienced personnel. The young officer, tall and thin-faced, has a watchful air as if feeling his way through alien territory.

Next to him stands a shorter individual, ruddy faced, apparently proud to be in his uniform, yet his stance reveals an awkwardness, as if unsure whether he has yet earned the right to wear the distinguished stripes of an officer. A mature-looking lieutenant commander – the wrinkles at the corners of his eyes a legacy, no doubt, of staring at countless horizons – converses courteously with the younger men. The lieutenant commander demonstrates naval urbanity in the finest tradition, but perhaps the sub-lieutenants seem a little intimidated. How do they regard the wardroom, with its deference to age-old customs? Do the young officers see the ambience as stuffy or outdated, like a pre-war London club?

The lieutenant ponders that when he had joined the Royal Navy ten years ago, he had witnessed disturbances at Invergordon which seemed to reflect the world's changing attitudes. The navy had been caught up in the course of social upheaval, the complex cause and effect that followed the disintegration of Victorian values.

His thoughts are interrupted by his neighbour: "Damn silly nonsense if you ask me," mutters the sub-lieutenant. "You hack around a golf course, chase after a small white ball, waste hours in the process, and all for what? Should be banned in my opinion along with all that stuff about cleeks, mid-irons, birdies, niblicks, nashie-mashie potatoes or whatever it is. It's enough to make you feel weak at the knees. The golfers with their fancy shoes and namby-pamby breeches should be buried deep inside their sand bunkers along with the rest of..."

"I enjoy a good round of golf," says a nearby commander. He leans towards the group.

"Splendid game!" cries the sub-lieutenant. "So stimulating, I'm sure, and such an intellectual challenge. I wish I had time for a quick round myself."

"Talking of quick rounds," says the commander, "mine's a half."

"Yes, sir, of course," says the sub-lieutenant. "Would you prefer a pint?"

"If you insist, my lad."

While the duly-humbled sub-lieutenant attends to the commander's drink (and those of the rest of the group), Lieutenant Sutton notices the easement of numbers within the anteroom. As officers start to wend their way towards the dining room, among them are the 'Wavy Navy' men, some of whom look young enough to be still at school. Their expressions remain serious and he wonders if the young men appreciate that tensions within the wardroom are felt by all, and that the ready switch from seriousness to light-heartedness does not demean the officers' strong and subtle dedication. He hopes the young officers see the banter as a means to assuage larger worries, like the ship's approach to the Island of Pantelleria, and the potential threat of the Luftwaffe's presence outlined by the commander earlier in the day.

As he peers across the anteroom, the lieutenant catches sight of the ship's padre and he notes the way in which the Reverend Henry Lloyd's cheerful voice lifts the spirits of those around him. Tomorrow, the padre will make use of the ship's tannoy system to keep the ship's crew informed of proceedings "...a bomb is falling and I think it is going to miss our port quarter – yes – (BOOM!) it has." During desperate moments, many of *Illustrious*'s crew members will discover that the padre's voice is the one thing that helps to keep insanity at bay.

Just now, however, the officers of HMS *Illustrious* face a more immediate development. While officers begin to make their way towards the dining room, Lieutenant Sutton and his squadron colleagues decide to join them. Suddenly, however, the plans of all are interrupted when crew members react to naval training and begin to rush towards their allotted posts as the 'action stations' klaxon is sounded. This is the moment, thinks the lieutenant while he joins others who dash along passageways, through still-open watertight doors, and up ladders. Now it begins.

6

Going Wrong

Dawn on Friday, 10th January 1941, reveals to the crewmen a generally fine Mediterranean day, the weak winter sunshine veiled by patchy layers of cloud. Following last night's rush of activity when hands were piped to action stations, the subsequent response resulted in a few skirmishes against the Italian Regia Aeronautica, but these were relatively minor. Fulmar fighter aircraft from 806 Squadron kept Italian reconnaissance and other aircraft at bay when they ventured close to the carrier, but the efforts of the Italians seemed sporadic and somewhat half-hearted. There was no sign of Luftwaffe activity during the night, and as a result the dark hours had proved quieter than expected.

In order to allow a reasonable period of rest for his crew, Captain Boyd eventually gave orders that personnel should be stood down from action stations, although anti-aircraft gunners were instructed to man their stations through the night. At present, Lieutenant Sutton joins a number of aircrew congregated on the ship's quarter-deck before breakfast.

Pleasantries are exchanged, then conversations become intermittent when the officers attempt to soak up the warmth of the early sun, still low in the sky. As they breathe in the brisk sea air and as they placidly contemplate the Mediterranean streams, perhaps some of the officers have feelings of guilt at the scenario before them; uncannily benign and in sharp contrast to the harsh winter scenes described in letters from home. The hardships of blackout and blitz endured by relatives seem distant in the present early-morning calm. Furthermore, the hazards of the Regia Aeronautica appear, one way or another, to be not so menacing – maybe fairly manageable – as was proved by the events of last night.

The Luftwaffe's looming threat seems of lesser significance just now and it's quite possible, think some of the officers, that the problems have been overstated. Certainly, the powers-that-be within the Admiralty and the Air Ministry appear convinced that the presence of the Luftwaffe will make little difference to the current threat. Perhaps lulled by such thoughts, the officers stare carelessly at the picturesque seas, the tranquil surroundings, and dawn hues. The prevalent air of quiet confidence may be enhanced for some by the sense of solidity provided by the flight deck structure directly above their heads.

In company with the *Illustrious*, a number of ships can be observed from the carrier's quarter-deck. As part of Operation Excess, the *Illustrious* steams in convoy with the Mediterranean Fleet's Force A which currently includes Admiral Cunningham's flagship, the Queen Elizabeth class battleship HMS *Warspite* with a displacement of 30,600 tons, and her fellow battleship HMS *Valiant*. Also in company are the destroyers HMS *Dainty*, HMS *Gallant*, HMS *Greyhound*, HMS *Griffin*, HMS *Jervis*, HMS *Juno*, HMS *Mohawk* and HMS *Nubian*.

With such a potent force around them, the officers on the *Illustrious*'s quarter-deck feel additionally reassured about the carrier's ability to resist and repel enemy raiders. The officers realise, of course, that there is no place for complacency and that, indeed, a busy flying programme has been organised for the day ahead. Nonetheless, perhaps some are lured into false senses of security as they gaze with admiration at the carrier's giant wake piled astern. They observe, too, the throw of white spume from the bow wave of the destroyer HMS *Gallant*, at present a few miles away as she attempts to catch up her station on the carrier's port quarter.

Force A, now positioned to the north-west of Malta, has negotiated hazardous waters during the night. However, optimism about the immediate future is reinforced by the knowledge that soon, as the ships steam towards their rendezvous point with Forces B and F and a number of merchantmen from Gibraltar, they will be part of an even more powerful convoy.

Officers realise, though, that these good omens should be tempered by the ship's less than ideal position, now within reach of enemy airfields in Sicily. In the opinion of many, a more prudent plan would have been to operate the aircraft carrier at a distance from the rest of the fleet. This, however, has been discounted in view of Admiral Cunningham's insistence that the *Illustrious* should remain at the heart of his fleet, that the carrier's presence boosts the morale of others in the fleet.

Officers therefore trust that the rendezvous will materialise without mishap, after which Operation Excess should be able to proceed with due dispatch. This should help to mitigate the difficulties created by the recent violent weather in the vicinity of Gibraltar, storm-force winds which have delayed the operation with its supplies so vital to the beleaguered island of Malta.

The battleship HMS *Renown* was severely damaged by the heavy seas, although the ship managed to limp into Gibraltar for urgent repairs. Less fortunate was the fate of a cargo ship driven onto rocks by the strength of the wind. Evidently the storm had its epicentre close to the Cape of Trafalgar, just forty or so nautical miles north-west of Gibraltar. Such storms, the lieutenant reflects, typified those of the southern reaches of the Bay of Cádiz, a sea area notorious for weather conditions feared by seafarers through the ages.

The lieutenant remembers naval conversations about the hurricane that blew up after the Battle of Trafalgar and how, to this day, the mayhem created by that hurricane remained the subject of contentious debate. Further losses of men and material had led to renewed suffering amongst fleets already devastated by the demands of the battle. Hundreds of sailors, amongst them individuals still recovering from their battle injuries, had died in the storm-tossed seas that followed the 21st October 1805.

Before the battle, however, the seas were uncannily calm and it was in a place not so very far from his present position, recalls the lieutenant, that a sixteen-year-old midshipman, Hercules Robinson from Dublin, stood on the poop deck of his ship HMS *Euryalus* to note the… 'beautiful misty sun-shiny morning of 21st October, the sea like a mill-pond but with an ominous ground-swell rolling in from the Atlantic'. Preparations for the fateful encounter began at once although it took all morning for the ships of both sides to inch their way into position.

When battle commenced, only half of the ships on either side would become engaged. Before long, with the action focused around the left of the French and Spanish line's centre, crews struggled to differentiate between friend and foe in the banks of gun smoke. Despite being choked and blinded by the smoke, officers continued to pace the decks boldly. At around a quarter past one, Admiral Nelson and Captain Hardy walked together on the quarter-deck of Nelson's flagship, HMS *Victory*. Hardy, a little ahead, turned to walk back but suddenly, through the fumes and the fog, he could see that Nelson had fallen. Hardy rushed forward. Something had gone badly wrong. Adjacent screams and explosions were heard…

"Look!" An officer on HMS *Illustrious*'s quarter-deck shouts and points with one hand.

"My God!"

"What's happened?" Men crane their necks as they stare aft.

"Are there any aircraft in the vicinity?" All peer up into the sky.

"Nothing obvious!"

"What could have happened then?"

"She was steaming fast – too fast to have been torpedoed."

The Mediterranean Fleet's rendezvous with Forces B and F (commanded by Rear-Admiral Renouf) has coincided with the closing moments of a forty-minute clash between Italian torpedo boats and Renouf's convoy. One Italian torpedo boat has been sunk, another has escaped. However, while the Mediterranean Fleet manoeuvred to take up station astern Rear-Admiral Renouf's convoy, and while the destroyer HMS *Gallant* tried to move to her new screening position, she was hit. Men now stare in awe at the *Gallant*'s collapsed bow wave, at the turmoil of phosphorescence which marks the surface around her hull. Within the hull, sixty men lie dead, twenty-five wounded.

"She must have hit a mine." The officers continue to gaze helplessly at the scene. The *Illustrious* begins a slow turn to starboard while destroyers race to the aid of their fellow ship. The aircrew on the quarter-deck abandon the area as they hasten to their places of duty.

On his flagship, Admiral Cunningham witnesses the drama through binoculars: 'I suddenly saw a heavy explosion under *Gallant*'s bows. She had been mined, and in water through which the battle-fleet had passed only a short time before.' The admiral will remember this as the moment at which the fortunes of his fleet began to change. Later, the ruddy-faced, grim-mouthed admiral who joined the Royal Navy forty-three years ago in 1898, and who has pronounced 'duty as the first business of a sea officer', will encapsulate this as the point at which 'things started to go wrong'.

Things, indeed, are about to go badly awry.

7

Trapani, Sicily

Major Walter Enneccerus of the Luftwaffe frowns as he peers up into the Sicilian sky. Just now he stands alone at the Italian Regia Aeronautica's airbase at Trapani on the north-west corner of the island. Despite his seeming anxiety, the major, in truth, has a sense of quiet confidence. He started early this morning, ahead of his colleagues, in order to prepare briefings for the operational mission planned for later in the morning. Now, with his preparations complete, the major can appreciate a few moments to himself before the arrival of the other squadron aircrew, pilots and rear-gunners.

As he watches squadron engineering personnel hasten with typical efficiency to prepare aircraft for the forthcoming mission, he contemplates with satisfaction his squadron's recent change of situation. When orders were received from the Oberkommando der Wehrmacht for the implementation of Operation Mittelmeer (the relocation of General Geisler's Fliegerkorps X), units had geared up with impressive speed for the move south.

Personnel had greeted Stuka Geschwader 3's transfer with particular enthusiasm. Expressions on the faces of the men of his own squadron – Geschwader 1 Stuka 2 – had reflected their thoughts. Even though the move would take place over the Christmas period, the announcement of the news seemed to be accepted by most as a welcome opportunity, a stroke of good luck, and an unexpected one at that. The squadron would exchange the bleakness of a dreary winter in northern climes for the temperate conditions of a Mediterranean island controlled by an Axis ally.

Not that their present situation, muses the major, is without its perils. British naval forces in the area, with their reputation for aggression and intransigence, were dominant in the Mediterranean theatre of operations and this, he realises, was the reason behind the Fliegerkorps' relocation.

Last November's action by the British against the Italian Fleet in harbour at Taranto had provided, in all probability, the final impetus for the execution of Operation Mittelmeer. When the major and his colleagues had learned about the events at Taranto, their sense of astonishment was shared, no doubt, by the hierarchy at Oberkommando der Wehrmacht.

The British had accomplished a masterstroke: the Royal Navy's aircraft carrier *Illustrious* had steamed sufficiently near to the 'heel' of Italy to allow the launch of British Swordfish aircraft – such antiquated machines – and the result had been remarkable...an unmitigated disaster from the Italian perspective. Taranto's harbour defences were caught off-guard; virtually half the Italian Fleet had been written off and the Italians were completely outwitted. The whole exercise was a shambles, and a complete farce from the German point of view. The major shakes his head; he wonders, sometimes, about his country's so-called ally. As far as he could perceive, the Italian approach to the war seemed to be ineffectual, at times almost half-hearted. What, he asks himself, will be the practical implications of operating with such an ally?

Major Enneccerus ponders the picture attached to one wall in the squadron's temporary office behind him. The picture portrays an unsmiling impression of the Italian leader Benito Mussolini, the *Duce*. The major is aware of rumours that the Luftwaffe's most senior officer, Field Marshal Göring, and the *Duce* do not see eye to eye; and that the Italian leader has described the field marshal as 'flashy and pretentious'. That's a bit rich, thinks the major. What about his own attire, not to mention the way the fellow struts around?

The major recalls the furore stirred up a couple of years before the war, when the Italian leader had paid a formal visit to Germany. The *Duce*'s uniform (so magnificent) was designed, it was said, especially for the occasion and his entourage were caparisoned with equivalent, or nearly the same, splendour. While he waited in Munich to greet his guest, Herr Hitler had worn the brown shirt and tunic and black trousers of the Nazi uniform. Munich's streets and those of Berlin were lined with troops, the buildings emblazoned with giant Nazi flags and brightly-coloured bunting. An eager population had welcomed the Italians; the Italian leader had delivered rousing speeches including an ovation to nearly 1,000,000 Berliners gathered on the Maifeld.

Of course, the wet weather and Field Marshal Göring's behaviour before the rally had hardly helped to placate the *Duce* or to put him in a good mood. There were reports that the field marshal's pet lion had upset the Italian by jumping up at him, and that Göring had delayed the proceedings by insisting that he played with an electric train set until the last minute. Major Enneccerus sighs: a pet lion; an electric train set enjoyed by the head of the Luftwaffe? Oh well, he ruminates, best not to dwell on such matters. Anyway, he resumes his line of thought, the *Duce* had surmounted the setbacks; he had appeared before the massive crowds and the people had roared approval, especially as he pronounced through the crackly loudspeakers: "When Fascism has a friend, it will march with that friend to the last." The tour had been an outstanding success, described by his son-in-law Count Galeazzo Ciano in glowing terms: 'The *Duce's* magnetism, his voice, his impetuous youthfulness completely captivated the German crowds.'

Perhaps the German people might have been less enthusiastic if they had learned about some of the *Duce*'s subsequent comments. Two or so years after the Italian leader's visit to Germany, Field Marshal Göring had gone to Rome to give an account of German preparations for war. The Polish question evidently became one of contentious debate which persisted for a number of months. The major knew of rumours that Count Ciano had warned his father-in-law not to trust the Germans. There were reports, too, that the *Duce*'s initial reaction of agreement with this advice had been swiftly modified when he announced that: 'honour compelled him to march with the Germans and that, anyway, he wanted his part of the booty.'

It seemed that when the *Duce* was in the presence of Germans he liked to thrust out his jaw, to compose his features to reflect an image of rock-like sternness, to speak with admiration of the German people's 'fine martial spirit' and their 'heroic philosophy'. However, there was hearsay within the Luftwaffe that the *Duce* was prone to tergiversation, and that behind their backs he described the Germans as 'merely soldiers, not real warriors', that he had spoken dismissively of German folk: 'Give them enough sausage, butter, beer and a little car and they won't worry about sticking bayonets into people.' Damnable cheek!

Then there's all this talk of extra-marital relationships. Major Enneccerus and his colleagues are aware of gossip about the Italian leader's association with women, and that he seeks the company of prostitutes. He also has a mistress, Claretta Petacci. The way they met was an intriguing episode.

Evidently she was the wife of an Italian air force lieutenant, and the story goes that she was amongst a crowd gathered by the roadside to greet the *Duce* as he drove by. Sitting in the back of his chauffeur-driven Alfa Romeo, he had taken note of the pretty girl with long straight legs and shapely breasts as she waved and shouted: *"Duce! Duce!"* He had immediately ordered his driver to stop the car. Benito Mussolini had stepped grandly out of his Alfa Romeo, paused, waved to the assembled masses, and strolled back towards the girl. Surrounding crowds had become hushed, bemused. The girl had trembled with excitement.

At a glance, the *Duce* had taken in the large green eyes framed around a handsome face. He had spoken a few words; her voice, when she replied, was delightfully husky. He had lingered to observe the tightly-curled black hair, the fussily attractive clothes. He had noticed that her upper lip was short, her teeth small; when she smiled, she revealed her gums. More words were spoken; arrangements were made. The relationship developed.

According to hearsay, Claretta Petacci would visit the *Duce* at the Palazzo Venezia. She would enter discreetly by a side door, then take a lift to an upper floor flat. The *Duce* would see her, sometimes for just a few minutes. The couple's love-making, so it was said, would be urgent, then he would leave, hastily adjusting his clothes as he returned for his next interview on weighty state matters.

Major Enneccerus glances at the surrounding Sicilian countryside. He takes a satisfied gulp of the fresh air. Even in January, the local climate seems favourable although he realises that there are traps for the unwary. Consider, for example, the fickle nature of indigenous winds. Just the other day, when squadron personnel were briefed on general local aspects, the *hauptmann* from the meteorological department had talked about the hazards of the gregale (the Greek wind) that blew out of the Balkans across the Ionian sea towards Sicily

When the *hauptmann* pointed to lines and ominous squiggles on his chart, the fellow attempted to describe the depression impetus needed to generate the necessary forces for the initiation of a powerful gregale – it was something like that, anyway. He then got quite carried away as he went on to describe the masterly mistral that would roar south from the Rhone valley, the hot and humid Levanter that blew off the Algerian coast to drive due west towards Gibraltar, and the hot and iniquitous sirocco and the khamsin winds that blew off the African coast.

The major checks his watch. Before long, the atmosphere will change to one of hectic activity when other squadron aircrew arrive. The briefings for this morning's operation can commence at that stage. In his mind, Major Enneccerus recaps his prepared details for the briefing and for the subsequent mission: technical data; local notes; intelligence update; meteorological prognosis. He observes the activities of the squadron engineers as they manoeuvre and line up dozens of Stuka Ju 87B aircraft. He gazes with a sense of admiration at the no-nonsense profile of the machines, the inverted gull-shaped wings, the long noses that house a single 880kW Jumo 211 Da engine, the distinctive Perspex hood above the pilot's and rear-gunner's cockpits, the fixed undercarriage, and the special wheel covers above each main wheel.

Of all the aircraft in the Luftwaffe's inventory, the major reckons that the Ju 87 must stand out as the most significant in the role of *Sturzkampfflugzeug*. How far-sighted of General Udet when he pressed the hierarchy to opt for the machine. Apart from anything else, consider the impact of the sirens fitted to those wheel covers. The terrifying wail of the sirens has a remarkable effect: enemy troops and civilians alike appear to lose their senses in panic; the influence on hearts and minds, and the sudden shattering of morale seems almost as useful as the bombs themselves. So much so that nowadays even the bombs have been fitted with fins to produce an unnerving and eerie whistle.

The major watches the squadron armourers as the men manoeuvre specialist trolleys to load the bombs for this morning's mission. Today will require the 'big one': a single 500kg bomb clamped to the central fuselage section of each aircraft. As an alternative, other combinations of bomb types can be fitted to racks under the aircraft wings.

There's little doubt that today's main target will demand every bit of attainable clout that the Luftwaffe can muster, and every bit of available skill from his squadron crews. Today's planned victim will be a different proposition altogether to that of the British aircraft carrier *Courageous*, torpedoed by a German U-boat in the early stages of the war. The major recollects the day when the news of the *Courageous*'s fate was announced, how this was greeted with elation in Germany. The U-boat skipper was awarded the Iron Cross, and his crewmen were treated like heroes. There were reports that when the *Courageous* was torpedoed, the ship had rolled so rapidly towards an angle so alarming that it was obvious to all that she was sinking fast.

The U-boat skipper had observed through his periscope as the port side of the flight-deck hung a few feet above the sea's surface, like some child's plaything suspended on strings. Ship's boats, swept from their stowages, were seen to burst through the sea to meet the turmoil of phosphorescence around the carrier's hull. Within the hull, the scenes could be imagined as aircraft trapped inside the hangar deck slid against others, adding to the ship's uneven top-weight. The carrier's list, further exaggerated as equipment and furniture broke loose from deck fastenings, became gradually more pronounced. The U-boat skipper had watched as a developing slick of oil and contaminants revealed that tanks had burst, and containers had fractured.

Men were hurled into the sea from all parts of the ship. Individuals were sucked from underwater compartments, then forced to struggle through strong undercurrents and polluted waters to reach the surface. The major had heard reports of a mast aerial that had fallen across a lanyard, and this had operated the ship's steam siren situated on the side of the funnel.

As with the morale-shattering impact of the sirens fitted to the Ju 87, evidently the mournful and non-stop blast of the *Courageous*'s steam siren had destroyed men's spirits. It was said that individuals listened with despair to what sounded like the carrier's final pleas before being sent to the deep. The *Courageous* had sunk within twenty minutes and apparently some 500 men had gone down with the ship.

However this morning's main target will need to be tackled with novel, nefarious techniques. The primary object of his squadron's mission boasts features which were not available to the British ship *Courageous*. The aircraft carrier *Illustrious* is modern, with well trained crews on up-to-date equipment. From the intelligence information gathered by the Luftwaffe, the major knows that the *Illustrious* has the advantage of radar-guided fighters as well as potent anti-aircraft armament and armour-plated decking. The fighters are a particular worry for Major Enneccerus. He and his men realise that a key weak point of their Ju 87 is the machines' vulnerability to enemy fighters. The aircrew have been briefed on the Fairey Fulmar fighters carried on the *Illustrious*, including the fact that in a six-week period last autumn, the Fulmars of the 806 Squadron had shot down ten Italian bombers.

When the Ju 87 crews attack the *Illustrious* they will have to confront robust fighter aircraft which, unlike those weird Swordfish aircraft, are of all-metal stressed skin construction. Luftwaffe intelligence has reported that the Fulmar is a two-seat monoplane powered by a single Rolls-Royce Merlin engine of 1,035 British horsepower, and that the aircraft carries eight fixed British Browning machine guns mounted in the wings.

Major Enneccerus sneaks another glance at his watch. He feels at once calm and anxious. His aircrew colleagues should arrive quite soon now. As commander II of Luftwaffe Geschwader 1 Stuka 2, he has onerous responsibility but he is an experienced aviator and he is well equipped to carry out his job. The major will be proud to lead his squadron when the Ju 87 machines are launched for the morning's mission. The major has been briefed by his superiors; soon he will pass on a stark message issued by General Geisler himself. In Major Enneccerus's view, the gist of the message was unequivocal – admirably so – and, indeed, a model of military brevity: Illustrious,' said the general, *'mussen sinken.'*

8

Rising Tension

As he stands within the bridge area of HMS *Illustrious*, the commander currently on duty looks uneasy. He glances at the telephone receiver in his hand before, with care, he returns the instrument to its cradle. Now he glances in turn at the personnel on the bridge, including the two senior officers present, Rear-Admiral Lyster and Captain Boyd. When he perceives the expression on the captain's face, the commander falters. With his characteristic air of phlegmatic calm, Captain Boyd, at first glance, appears reasonably unruffled. However, thinks the commander, perhaps the sanguine impression is, just this once, somewhat deceptive. The commander reflects that so far today, the captain, together with his fellow crew members, have been kept in a state of what you might call... well...quite useful employment.

Earlier that morning, when the destroyer HMS *Gallant* had struck a mine, all who watched the event experienced a sudden sense of foreboding. As the horror of the incident began to unfold, the flow of messages from HMS *Warspite* reflected the commander-in-chief's understandable agitation. Admiral Cunningham ordered the rapid re-disposition of his ships; the destroyer HMS *Mohawk* was instructed to take the *Gallant* in tow; HMS *Griffin* was told to stand by. Rear-Admiral Renouf was directed to cover the procedures when – as the commander-in-chief said – 'what remained of HMS *Gallant*' was hauled towards Malta.

Troubles then began to mount. While HMS *Mohawk* manoeuvred into position, she was attacked by two Italian SM 79 aircraft. HMS *Bonaventure* and HMS *Griffin* immediately opened fire on the Italian raiders. The latter dropped their torpedoes prematurely, then retreated. Italian high-level bombers appeared on the scene, but these were kept at bay by prodigious levels of anti-aircraft fire from British ships. As the morning progressed, Swordfish anti-submarine patrols were launched and a number of the

Fulmar aircraft from *Illustrious* were scrambled to provide fighter cover.

Now, as the time approaches midday, the commander and others on the bridge have additional worries. These were highlighted by the announcement some thirty minutes earlier of a new and alarming development. A signals officer and a petty officer, both breathless with excitement, caused a sudden hush on the bridge as they announced that a special message was about to come through. Even the unflappable Captain Boyd appeared apprehensive. The urgent news, when it was delivered, indicated that intelligence code-breakers had intercepted German wireless traffic.

Intelligence staff warned that the Luftwaffe had plans for air raids against the Mediterranean Fleet and these were due to take place sometime today. As yet, however, there was no indication of the scale of the planned attack, and there was no intimation of the intended target. Captain Boyd, having absorbed the implications of the message, merely shrugged his shoulders: his ship's personnel were at action stations already; he and his crewmen were as prepared as they could be. Privately, though, individuals began to wonder what, exactly, was likely to be in store for them.

In addition to the tension stirred up by the morning's escalating and hectic activity, personnel were still shaken by the repercussions of HMS *Gallant*'s mining. Men speculated on the possible outcome as the stricken destroyer was dragged towards safety at Malta. Zigzag patterns carved in the sea around the *Gallant* could be made out while escort ships tried to shield their protégé. All who observed the painful process did so with trepidation. Progress at the gentle speed of just five knots appeared agonisingly slow.

At present, however, the crew of HMS *Illustrious* see the *Gallant* and her escorts fade gradually into the distance. The carrier steams towards Malta in the wake of Force B, Force F and four merchantmen. This convoy, which has assumed a south-easterly course and which is currently some 100 nautical miles from Malta, plans to reach the island by teatime. The commander's involuntary sigh of relief is apparent as he ponders the forthcoming and welcome haven offered by Malta.

As with most experienced naval men, he has close knowledge of the island, the areas of creeks which include French Creek and the intricate series of natural harbour basins within Grand harbour. He pictures the island's historic naval heritage typified by French Creek, so named after Napoleon's ships were anchored there. The dictator, anxious to annex Malta, had asked the island's grand master to provide fresh water for warships. The grand master, though, had refused and within twenty-four hours, Napoleon had captured the islands. As a consequence, the grand master (a German called Von Lompesch) became the last man in history to carry the title.

The commander tries to imagine the present levels of activity in and around the complexities of Grand harbour. Within the harbour area and spilling into the streets of the adjacent Maltese capital of Valetta will be, he assumes, an air of urgency, a non-stop rush of movement. Crowded with exotic classes of vessel, the surrounding waters will be filled with forests of masts, curious clatters, crashes and commotion, and ubiquitous gulls which, as if to clear a pathway, will cross and re-cross the hulls of vessels on the move. There will be naval parties and dockyard workers, individuals who hurry hither and thither, towards dockside huts, storerooms, warehouses and men who, in their impatience, kick aside discarded warps, battered cans, fishermen's debris, general flotsam.

On a fiercer front, citizens will have to contend with the hazards of Italian air raids, the effects of petrol rationing, food shortages, and countless more difficulties. He has heard about the stoicism and ingenuity of the Maltese people. Native fortitude has been helped by natural assets which include large underground shelters in the area of Birzebbuga and elsewhere. If the Maltese population has learned to live with the problems of war, the commander has heard, too, that local folk are indebted to the support of the British, that co-operation and pluck have helped to resolve fearful predicaments, and save many lives.

Of course the co-operation between the Maltese and the British is of mutual benefit and the island's history of coping with conflict is legendary. This is revealed by the military-like structures in and around Valetta, the towering fortifications of Floriana, the grandeur of Fort Saint Elmo at the tip of the peninsular bordered by Grand harbour to the south, Marsamxett harbour to the north. The first British docks, installed at Fort Saint Michael in the early part of the nineteenth century and allotted the somewhat unglamorous title of 'Dock Number One', had acted through the decades as the British Fleet's headquarters. From the British perspective, Malta's ability to provide deep water facilities for warships had made the island a place of strategic significance.

Moreover, the accessibility of the town of Valetta offers popular opportunities to crew members. Valetta boasts clubs and bars, red light areas and numerous hotels, some a little eccentric, some distinctly dubious. The town's reputation for prolific numbers of prostitutes (more, apparently, per head of population than most other ports in Europe) is famed amongst seafarers. The whorehouses at the back of the dock area are readily available and the occupants could seem as diverse as the harbour's anomalous mix of vessels. The emphasis is international; many of the women are voluptuous Orientals, a type much favoured by seamen.

The ship's gossip after a visit to Malta could be intriguing.

"Sir!" A petty officer points, with an outstretched hand, to draw the commander's and others' attention to Fulmar aircraft on the horizon. Bridge personnel have received reports that two Italian aircraft have been shot down by Fulmars, and now the fighters will return to refuel and rearm. This means that the recent lulls in bridge activity will have been short-lived, so typical of the ups and downs of this day. He is conscious that things will start to hot up again quite soon and that bridge activity will resume a frenetic pace at any time.

From his personal perspective, the commander reckons he is lucky to have a man of Lieutenant Alfie Sutton's experience as an extra pair of hands to help out with bridge duties. The lieutenant, who has been made available for such duties owing to his temporary inability to fly, has been sent away for an early lunch in the wardroom. However, he will be of invaluable assistance when he returns before long.

The Fulmars are observed closely as they set up for their approach to the *Illustrious*. The deck landing officer – Lieutenant 'Haggis' Russell – stands in his allotted spot with yellow signal bats at the ready. Maintainers and armament specialists stand by. Other crews are poised to handle the aircraft when the machines have been slowed by arrester wires slung across the flight deck. On the bridge, officers focus their binoculars and stare purposefully. Just now, some of these officers may have satisfactory, if transitory, senses of calm. Suddenly, though, this is shattered by an imperative cry on the bridge: "Hostile aircraft, sir…two of them…due south, very low level…headed this way…"

Events happen with practised and professional proficiency. Captain Boyd orders the carrier to be swung out of line, anti-aircraft fire opens up and two Italian SM 79s are seen to release their torpedoes. The carrier is manoeuvred robustly while torpedo tracks are observed to pass to one side. The Fulmar fighters are then instructed to chase the enemy aircraft.

As the Fulmars give chase, officers watch the SM 79s drop down to very low level. The machines skim above the sea's surface, and jink vigorously as they head north towards the Sicilian coast on the far horizon. When the aircraft disappear from sight, the commander on the bridge notes the development of another pause in proceedings. He realises that in this see-saw day of changing fortunes, the quiet spells – as if to mark the lull before a storm – add a poignant dimension to the air of rising tension. He sees Captain Boyd glance up at the now-empty sky, then at his watch (the time is just before 1230 hours), then at the carrier's flight deck.

The captain monitors a sub-flight of Fulmars and some Swordfish aircraft which have been brought up from the hangar deck to the flight deck. The machines are now ranged, their engines warmed up ready for take-off. All on the bridge sense the captain's quandary as he ponders an immediate predicament. The machines are due to take off at 1235 hours precisely, after which other aircraft will return from patrol and begin their approaches to land. Captain Boyd would like to order the ranged aircraft airborne immediately, but this would mean turning the carrier into wind. He has instructions from Admiral Cunningham that such a turn is forbidden without prior permission. In just over five minutes time, pre-arranged permission will be granted automatically and the captain, no doubt, is reluctant to seek early authority from the already-harassed admiral.

The commander spots the captain check his watch once more. The time is now just past 1230 hours. An air of growing suspense is palpable. The restlessness of the aircrews in their Swordfish and Fulmars ranged on the flight deck can be imagined; the pilots are seen to stare up at the carrier's island as if willing the captain into action. 'Haggis' Russell, too, has an aura of impatience: he stands stoically in his special protective clothing, his yellow signal bats at the ready. Occasionally, the deck landing officer is seen to turn and look behind him as he searches surrounding airspace. From time to time, other crewmen also glance up to check the skies. All, however, remain in their briefed positions. All watch; all must wait.

Another minute ticks by, then another. At 1234, Captain Boyd at last delivers the yearned-for order and the carrier commences a turn into wind. Within a minute or so, the deck landing officer receives the required signal from the bridge. This is passed to the first of the ranged aircraft and the machine is then seen to roar down the carrier's flight deck. As other aircraft follow, crew members on board HMS *Illustrious* perhaps heave private sighs of relief even though, at this instant, the men remain unaware that the final piece in a developing jigsaw of jeopardy is about to be placed.

"Radar report, sir," the voice of a duty rating pipes up. Officers swing round, stare at the horizon, frantically focus binoculars. "Aircraft formations, sir – large ones – approaching from a northerly direction."

9

Illustrious Looms

As Major Enneccerus and his rear gunner gaze at the ranks of aircraft that hold formation on their Ju 87B, the two men speculate, perhaps, on the potential power of the massed formations. The aircraft hold a loose battle formation as the Stuka Geschwader units cross the Val di Mazara area of Sicily, the machines now on a south-easterly heading towards their target. The greyish colour of their Luftwaffe paint-work makes ideal camouflage against the patchwork Sicilian background; the ominous-looking swastikas daubed on fuselages and wings add a finishing touch to a spectacle which is bound to strike fear into the hearts of the enemy. Some forty or so of these Stukas are supported by bombers and torpedo-droppers from the Regia Aeronautica.

The major glances to his left towards the eastern end of Sicily. He squints his eyes against the weak sun as he looks towards the area of Catania, the base for other units of Fliegerkorps X. To the north of Catania, he pictures the towering presence of Mount Etna but this is many kilometres away and hard to make out except when ambient conditions allow markedly good visibility. Between the major's aircraft and Catania, the hilly terrain is dotted with orange plantations, terraced vineyards, dense olive groves, and twisty roads that lead into the Sicilian villages.

Within these villages, poverty-stricken – or what appear to be – peasants have become adept at living lives of lazy inconsequence. The major imagines the village houses with their slogans in praise of '*Il Duce*' and he reflects on how recent events must have stirred dubious loyalty amongst the inhabitants. Maybe this is about to change and perhaps it is merely a matter of time before the Sicilians and their enigmatic society – such a stark contrast to the squadron's previous location – will revert to traditional values.

As he looks towards the Luftwaffe base at Catania, the major tries to envisage the habitat, still new to him just now, although he knows he will need, as swiftly as possible, to become familiar with local terrain. He pictures the confluence of waterways to the south of Catania, how these lead into the Gornalunga river, and how, north and south, various hilltop towns and villages are served by tortuous routes that ascend the slopes up to the main piazza, the Piazza del Mercato. The influence of the Mafia within the island is evident, the organisation's Sicilian origins go back to the Middle Ages. Nineteenth century absentee landlords engaged members of the Mafia to manage *latifundia* (landed estates) through intimidation, and now, even in wartime, the Mafia's influence remains significant.

Major Enneccerus has been made aware that the Mafia's manipulations combined with other local factors have created curious conflictions within Sicily's innately pessimistic and sceptical society. He understands that the populace who live near the Luftwaffe base at Catania can be subtly different to the folk adjacent to his own unit's base at Trapani. Even though his unit is new to the area, he has heard that some of his men already have attempted bold liaisons with local girls. While certain local attractions may be out of bounds to his men, nonetheless the frustrations of war, of military life, and lack of female company, will ensure that regulations are circumvented by the determined. It will not be long, he reckons, before some on his unit present him with predicaments which he, the exalted major, will be expected to resolve with some sort of magic wave of the wizard's wand.

As a Luftwaffe commanding officer, the major knows he is expected to show wise deliberation when he deals with his multiplicity of tasks. These, he well understands, include general factotum and counsellor to his men. He understands, too, that he will have particular difficulties when marital and related problems become involved. The married men on his squadron can be faced with harsh dilemmas. The wider world probably view the Stuka Geschwader personnel as ogres from some form of hideous extra-terrestrial outpost...sheer nonsense, of course, thinks the major. Certainly, his personnel are well qualified and well disciplined, nevertheless they are human beings, individuals assigned to a task and who, like everybody else in this war, have to obey orders.

"Look there, sir..." the major's rear gunner interjects. "We're closing on the target. We'll cross the coastline soon."

"Not long now," says the major. He glances across at the Ju 87B flown by a *kapitän*, a naval aviator of some experience and a most suitable man, to lead the other Stuka Geschwader on today's mission. In a couple of day's time, these leaders will be joined by another commander, Major Paul-Werner Hozzel. Major Hozzel will fly down from Lusterburg in East

Prussia and Major Enneccerus looks forward to briefing his friend and colleague on the outcome of today's operation. The time is now past midday, and in the distance a number of ships can be made out. There appear to be distinct clusters of vessels. At least, ponders Major Enneccerus, the Regia Aeronautica has been useful in that respect: regular reconnaissance reports by the Italians have been generally good and accurate.

As the view of the British ships materialises, in his mind Major Enneccerus runs through the procedures covered in his earlier aircrew briefing. The methods have been practised against a special mock-up target designed to simulate an aircraft carrier. The Luftwaffe tactics, based on Italian debriefs of British systems of air defence, will aim to divide the fire of the British ships.

Thirty or so Stukas have been ordered to concentrate on the *Illustrious*; these aircraft will break into three groups which will constantly change height and relative formation so as to confuse the enemy range-finders. The Stukas will peel off from different groups and directions in order to frustrate the ack-ack defences. Techniques have been devised so that no single machine will impede colleagues. Some of the aircraft will dive from 12,000 feet all the way down, others will check their descent at 7,000 feet before recommencing dives at angles between sixty-five and eighty degrees. Once the bombs have been released, crews will follow them down to the carrier's deck level where the Stukas will strafe the flight deck. Later, the result of this attack will be summarised by Admiral Cunningham. At once fascinated and appalled, the admiral described the moment when his fleet's aircraft carrier disappeared: 'in a forest of great bomb splashes...there was no doubt we were watching complete experts...we could not but admire the skill and precision of it all.'

Just now, though, as the Luftwaffe units cross the Sicilian coastline, the aircrews prepare themselves for what they hope will be a short, sharp operation. Cockpit procedures are checked and cross-checked. All eyes monitor the targets ahead. If Major Enneccerus has further conversations with his rear gunner, these must remain brusque, to the point. As they stare out of their Ju 87B cockpits, to these men – and to all of their fellow aircrew – the chief objective of their mission becomes gradually more obvious. HMS *Illustrious* looms. The profile of the aircraft carrier is unmistakable.

10

Stuka Intruder

A Swordfish pilot of 815 Squadron of His Majesty's Fleet Air Arm prepares to make his approach to land on the flight deck of the *Illustrious*. The time is a few minutes past 1235 hours on Friday, 10th January 1941, and the pilot's subsequent report follows:

'I was in the waiting position over the port quarter of *Illustrious* watching her turn into wind. She flew off the Swordfish for the anti-submarine patrols, and a gaggle of Fulmars. "Haggis" Russell, the deck landing officer, was in his accustomed position by the 4.5-inch gun turrets on the port side of the flight deck waving his yellow bats. I started my approach. As I turned gently to port with my arrester-hook down, Haggis suddenly disappeared from sight in a great burst of smoke from all the guns under his feet. I was not yet aware that anything was wrong: we often took off and landed with the ship's guns firing.

'Banking a little more to port, I straightened up to approach the round-down of the flight deck. I saw that the after lift was down. It would be up by the time I got there or Haggis would wave me round again. Suddenly, a strange aircraft came into view, flying from port to starboard, right in front of me, across the flight deck. Its huge swastika was painted red on the side of a grey fuselage. As I pressed the trigger of my Vickers gun, the Stuka was right ahead in my sights but it dipped – as though in salute – and dropped an enormous great bomb right down the after lift well which was still gaping.

'The bomb looked like a GPO pillar-box painted black. By the flames which shot out of the hole in the deck, I realised that it had exploded in the hangar. The lift itself burst out of the deck and shot a few feet into the air and sank back into the well...'

Just at this moment, Lieutenant Alan William Frank Sutton hastens towards the hangar deck as he makes for the carrier's bridge. Some half-an-hour ago, when the duty commander had suggested that the lieutenant should aim for an early lunch, the suggestion was accepted with due gratitude. He had joined a number of other aircrew members in the wardroom where their conversation, not unnaturally, had centred around the morning's activities. Now, though, the commander will anticipate his return and the lieutenant seems anxiously impatient as he hurries back to his place of duty. Sutton paces along a passageway towards a typical hangar deck scenario, a few aircrew who stand in various parts of the hangar are in animated discussion, maintainers who work to prepare aircraft for the flying programme and specialists who attend to the aircraft with their equipment are scattered around the hangar. A young midshipman sits patiently in his aircraft while he and his machine are raised to flight-deck level in the carrier's after lift. The lieutenant is about to enter the hangar deck when...

BOOM!

11

Hangar Horrors

Knocked down by the bomb blast, Lieutenant Sutton staggers to his feet. He searches himself for symptoms of injury, or signs of blood. He is aware of a few scratches and bruises and an involuntary tremble of his hands signifies the onset of shock, otherwise he finds himself to be pretty much unhurt.

The force of the blast has propelled him along a passageway and into an officers' accommodation area. As he glances back, he sees that he has been thrust past two still-open watertight doors, meaning any slight divergence of direction would have been fatal. He observes rows of cabin doors, some burst open by the bomb blast, some still closed. He can see no-one else in the immediate vicinity, although he is aware of unusual sounds not far off. He sniffs the air: an odious smell accompanies curls of smoke. As he wipes one sleeve across his forehead he realises that his clothing has been ripped and scorched. He tears away unwanted remnants then hastily adjusts his trousers. One glance at his shoes reveals that, remarkably, both seem intact and both remain securely fastened to his feet. He straightens up and decides to hurry towards the hangar, the source of the unusual sounds.

The lieutenant gasps at the sights when he enters the hangar: bodies lie scattered; aircraft have begun to burn; torpedoes and other live ammunition roll unchecked around the hangar confines. Noxious fumes from battery acid and from exploding cylinders permeate the atmosphere. Crates, spare aircraft engines, airscrews, and other specialist items have started to fall down from the supposedly-secure deck-head storage arrangements. Stanchions of tubular steel (about as thick as the average lamp-post) have been twisted into spirals, like ornamental toys. As bomb fragments and general wreckage careered across the area, scorching-hot splinters have killed or injured personnel who happened to be in the way.

Machine-gun ammunition within flame-engulfed aircraft has also begun to detonate and rebound in a lethal onslaught of projectiles around the enclosed space. In the after lift, the Fulmar aircraft and its young midshipman pilot have been overwhelmed by fire. In a bizarre moment, Lieutenant Sutton sees the new commanding officer of 815 Squadron, Lieutenant-Commander John de F Jago, gaze at the ground as if transfixed. The lieutenant-commander, at the instant of explosion, had stood in the centre of the hangar while he chatted with one of his aircrew colleagues, Lieutenant Kemp. Now the motionless lieutenant-commander stares in disbelief at the headless corpse by his feet.

At this stage, much-rehearsed Royal Navy training starts to take over. The fundamentals are straightforward: put out fires; rescue casualties; apply first aid. Fire and damage control parties have begun to appear and Lieutenant Sutton observes firemen race to deal with infernos. Nearby, he hears the sound of choking cries. As he moves across to help a man, he sees eyes that peer out from a blackened face, and a head that streams with blood. He notes the filthy, oil-soaked clothes, the uncontrolled shivers that now afflict the man's body. These symptoms hamper the lieutenant's attempts at injury assessment, as do the casualty's obvious signs of terror and bewilderment which inhibit any willingness to co-operate. As if to reinforce the burden of his plight, the man mouths pitiful, meaningless oaths. The lieutenant tries to ignore these while he bends to apply treatment to the lacerations around the man's face, the hair half-ripped from his scalp. As stretcher-bearers hasten to the scene, medical orderlies bring bandages and other first aid equipment.

When stretcher-bearers attempt to lift the man up, he lets out a scream. Soon, as he is rushed off to the medical centre for the attention of Surgeon-Commander Keevil, his shouts are joined by others. The noise assumes a tormented, animal-like howling. A voice, high-pitched in its anxiety, cries out: "My life-belt...my life-belt...I've lost my life-belt." To one side, a sudden crash reverberates as items tumble from deck-head mountings.

The lieutenant sees an injured maintainer trapped by heavy debris. A petty officer, backed by half a dozen ratings, races to the scene. He has to roar to make himself heard: "Come on now lads – heave!" In other areas, while crewmen charge to and fro, collisions occur as individuals blunder into one another. Fire-control parties scurry about, run out hoses, or yell instructions. When water is applied, the deck surface becomes a slimy conglomeration of oil and liquid, a dangerous mix to add to men's troubles. However, if there is an impression of panic, this is misleading: men's activities are driven by their instinctive reaction to danger, and to naval training.

He now checks for others in need of assistance. He spots a crewman who squats amongst debris as he nurses one of his arms. The crewman, still dazed from the speed of the disaster, sits in pathetic contemplation of his situation. His arm, half-torn from the shoulder socket, has been scalded by some acid-like substance. He mutters soft and fluent curses while he rocks back and forth. He grips his injured arm tenderly, as if to urge it better.

The lieutenant kneels beside the man before, as judiciously as possible, he tries to ease the victim's arm upwards and inwards, a vain attempt to reconnect the shoulder joint. The effort, however, brings a flood of angry curses. The lieutenant finds the acid-like substances on the victim's arm slippery and painful to handle and the man's oaths increase with each jolt and jar of his limb. When his pale face turns a greenish pallor and when, with his good hand, he squeezes his stomach, the lieutenant realises the man is about to retch.

Nearby, a stretcher-bearer cries: "Easy does it lads…that one's had it… leave him for now…we'll deal with it later." The lieutenant sees a corpse, eyes staring out, facial expression frozen at the instant of death. The young head jerks in time with the accidental movement of adjacent stretcher-bearers. As a patient is bundled onto a stretcher, his tenuous clutch on life is worsened when he attempts to cough up contaminants that burn and poison his intestines.

In another part of the hangar, the lieutenant glimpses a young rating who stares in stunned incredulity at the charred remains of a colleague. Evidently uncertain what to do, the rating glances up and down as if contemplating the placement of remains, section by section, into a nearby cardboard box. When the rating turns around to vomit, the lieutenant looks away.

While more rescue and damage control parties appear within the hangar deck, a new urgency possesses everyone present. Following the initial shock of surprise, the ship's company pull together in instinctive, well-drilled routines. Men understand that present actions will decide the carrier's fate, and a steely determination will be required if the enemy is not to prevail. Below decks, men listen to the padre's calm commentary from his position on the bridge. The voice of the Reverend Henry Lloyd over the ship's loudspeaker system helps men to realise that the ship is still under control, the captain remains at his post, assistance of some form or another will be forthcoming.

Hazards, however, persist. Difficulties within the hangar deck are exacerbated by the draft created by the carrier's forward speed. As the ship still steams at the speed needed for launching aircraft, an unwelcome rush of air fans the flames of hangar fires. Lieutenant Sutton hears a further series of crashes as equipment falls, ammunition explodes and the aircraft continue to burn. Above him, a shower of sparks is created when an electrical cable is severed. Overhead lights flicker ominously; dust from overhead pipe lagging floats down. The lieutenant, worried that his actions may aggravate cartilage and nerve damage to his patient's arm, reaches for an adjacent first aid kit then applies padded supports and bandages to restrict movement of the arm. Suddenly, the man's moans and curses are drowned by a shriek from close by. When the lieutenant glances up he sees a maintainer on his knees while he attends to an injured colleague. The maintainer cries: "He's stopped breathing!" At once, the lieutenant dashes across and places two fingers on the side of the casualty's neck to check for signs of pulse.

An instructor's image appears in his mind as he tries to recall the 'Schafer' method of resuscitation: *Firstly, place the patient face downwards on the ground.* What about other injuries? He catches sight of a bare bone protruding through the man's trouser leg. *Do not delay: to start artificial respiration procedures, position yourself to face the patient's head then place yourself astride his body, or to one side. Press your hands gently into the small of his back. Position your thumbs so each nearly touches the other, then spread your fingers on either side of the body over the lowest ribs.* The lieutenant checks the man's ribs. Are they broken? He thinks not. Thank God! Now what? *Lean forward and steadily allow the weight of your body to fall on the patient's ribs and so produce a firm downward pressure. On no account should this be violent. Continue to sway your body forward and backward upon your hands about twelve to fifteen times a minute without any marked pause between the movements.*

Before long, as these procedures produce a convulsion from the victim followed by a surge of watery vomit, the maintainer is instructed to take over. The lieutenant stands up, and turns around to return to his former patient. It must be hours, he thinks, since the bomb exploded. In truth, though, the hours have been a mere matter of minutes and further evidence of time's trickery becomes clear when efforts to reach his patient are interrupted by:

BOOM!

12

Concussed

Lieutenant Sutton's new situation is sudden and strange. He perceives a veil of blankness then obscure, indiscriminate images: an old man and his old companion – skeleton people – with tight yellow skin stretched across high cheekbones. The two old people move sluggishly back and forth. Neither of them speaks. A tall man with the same high cheekbones and with cropped black hair moves in the vicinity. He talks occasionally but with an accent that makes him hard to understand. He seems to work feverishly one minute, running about his tasks with a look on his face as if he expects time to stop before he is ready. Then he pauses and stands still, his black eyes sullen, hollow, haunted. He looks maltreated, ghostly, trapped in some foreign place.

Lieutenant Sutton, through the grey of concussion, sees a big house with broken windows unmended. He thinks that he would like to walk up to the house and repair the broken windows. The house seems terrifyingly exposed. An imagined knock at the front door receives no answer but it swings open. Inside, there is no movement, no sign of life. The kitchen is stark, the table has been laid; there are dishes on the table, bowls of porridge, fried eggs and sliced bread. On the food a little mould has started to form. A few flies buzz aimlessly about. A cobweb falls across his forehead and seems to try to restrain him.

Through the broken windows he sees how the garden has been neglected, how weeds have sprung up, and wild vines have twisted themselves into the branches of fruit trees. A young girl faces the house from the garden. Through her hair a breeze blows gently. Her hands are clenched by her side. Her blood-spattered feet are scratched and bare. When she falls, struck by bullets, swarms of people run towards her like a crazed mob. They run fast, crouching as they go, towards the tiny, pathetic bundle from which blood gushes onto her white print dress. He stares and stares and as he does he sees a centre of fire with a brilliant, white heat, shining bright without any colour.

His subliminal mind drifts unwillingly to the past, to his parents, to his father, to his father's war experiences. He senses other snatches of memory, of poignant words, of Rudyard Kipling's...*grant us strength to die!*...to die...strength to die...to die...

13

Heaven or Hell?

Die! Death? Dead? *Am I dead?* I feel as if I am; in fact, right now I feel like death warmed up. Where am I? Maybe I'm in heaven; I trust I'm not in the other place.

This, then, is what it must feel like to be in heaven. But I can sense a lot of pain, which doesn't seem exactly heaven-like. Perhaps this will take time to ease off. Apart from that, I suppose it's a case of…well, so far so good. I know that I should have done things very differently when I was alive, though. Looking back, there are many aspects of life that I now regret. I realise, for instance, that I should have done far more to help my fellow man, fewer things to help myself. I'm sure that I should have taken religion more seriously, I never could quite get to grips with all of the rigmarole. Pity really, but it's too late now, I suppose. At least Peggy has done well in that department. She's always been a staunch Roman Catholic. She was brought up as such. I've even seen proof of this in photographs of her as a pristine young Catholic girl in her pristine white dress on a beautiful Spanish day. Poor Peggy. Does she know?

But this heaven is a peculiar place, assuming I am in heaven, of course. There's a horrible stench everywhere, lots of moaning and shouting, and I can't see very well. My eyes seem glued together. Is that someone looking at me, I wonder who it can be? Peggy, perhaps? The duty angel? I'm sure I remember the padre talking about the duty angel last night. Was it last night?

"Sir! Oh, sir! What have they done to you?"

What a silly question! Who is that fellow?

"Sir! Oh, sir! Can you hear me?"

Yes, of course I can hear you. What do you take me for? A complete dolt? Maybe I should attempt to reply. That's not a bad idea. But how do

I speak? My mouth, my lips – my whole head – everything feels most odd. I'm sure I'm not myself. I'd better have a shot at talking, though; here goes... *"Whappening...?"*

"Sir! You look terrible!"

Terrible? That's bloody rude... Am I not a pretty sight? So I look terrible do I? In that case, perhaps I really *am* in the other place.

"Sir! Let me help you to sit up."

My God! I can see better now. This fellow's bathing my forehead. There's blood everywhere: foul, sticky stuff. I don't think I'm in heaven at all. I don't think that's the duty angel, I don't think it's Peggy, I don't think...I do think! In fact I'm sure it's...

"Marine Tregaskis!"

"Yes, sir. Take it easy, now. You've just had a very narrow escape."

14

Quarter-deck Mayhem

"Take it easy, sir," repeats Marine Tregaskis.

"Easy?" asks a dazed Lieutenant Sutton. "What do you mean easy?"

"Sorry, sir, no offence."

The lieutenant stares groggily at his marine servant. "You're a good fellow, Tregaskis," he says eventually. "You must have saved my life."

"That's okay, sir. But I've got to bind up that wound above your eyes, it's bleeding quite profusely. Hold still, please, while I try to sort it out."

As he finds his sight still impaired – affected, amongst other things, by a sensation of brilliant, aching lights – the lieutenant decides to remain seated and while he waits, he thinks further grateful thoughts about his overworked guardian angel. When his head injury has been duly bound, he indicates his willingness to attempt to stand up. Assisted to his feet by his marine servant, the lieutenant sways drunkenly as he tries to regain his bearings. He struggles to maintain his balance, and he blinks his eyes to rid them of an accumulation of blood. Despite difficulties he finds that a return to a state of reasonable consciousness is quite rapid, aided, perhaps, by his new and remarkable surroundings.

He is now in the open air and he stands on the quarter-deck of HMS *Illustrious*. He looks around anxiously, aghast at adjacent sights. Laid out in lines on the quarter-deck, he observes row upon row of men, casualties both alive and dead. The environment is dominated by a pall of thick black smoke that coalesces with surges of steam. The steam pours from a damaged fire main and further vapour is generated when fire-fighters' water touches the flight deck now heated by infernos in the hangar deck below.

The lieutenant hears men yell instructions while damage control parties rush to particular areas; he sees first aiders and stretcher-bearers, the men earnest in their efforts to help individuals on the quarter-deck.

Apprehensively, he listens to the low groans of injured men, individuals who thrash about restlessly, babble incoherently, their pain and discomfort all too evident.

"Shouldn't these casualties be taken to the wardroom?" the lieutenant's hoarse voice strives to make itself heard.

"That's not possible, sir," the marine servant shakes his head. "The wardroom's role as an emergency sick quarters has been…well, the wardroom itself has been smashed to pieces, sir. The last bomb…"

"The wardroom?"

"It's a horrifying scene down there, I'm afraid."

The lieutenant continues to sway uncertainly. He tries to imagine the present state of his naval 'home', the focus of his on-board social life, the centre of last night's cheerful conversations, a place of polished furniture, comfortable armchairs, and naval pictures…the place where he has just had his lunch. He scratches the back of his head as he hesitates but after a short pause he appears to make up his mind. He glances purposefully at his marine servant and says: "We'd better get down to work, Tregaskis."

"Are you sure you're feeling up to it, sir?"

"I don't think we've much choice, do you?"

The two men nod grimly, then separate as each searches for an injured shipmate in need of assistance. When he spots a man waving his hands in the air, the lieutenant grabs a first aid kit and hastens towards a rating who lies in a patch of putrid water coalesced with blood. The rating, placed next to corpses with canvas covers thrown roughly across, flails his severely burned hands in the air in vain attempts to soothe them. The lieutenant kneels down to inspect the man's hands. His attempts at injury assessment are hampered, however, by the rating's restless movements and by the reek of petroleum fuel from the man's torn boiler suit, a disagreeable addition to the surrounding stench of cordite and disinfectant.

The lieutenant tries to offer words of consolation but his patient's mumbled replies are exchanged for curses when first aid treatment is applied. At the sight of his own hands, the rating's look of dismay is accompanied by a gasp of fear and revulsion. "Steady, old chap," says the lieutenant. "This has to be done, I'm afraid, then the doctors can sort you out later."

Eventually, though, when the lieutenant has completed the treatment, he stands up to search for others in need of help. Momentary reflections on his own uncertain state of health cross his mind, but these have to be put aside as he spots further casualties brought up to the crowded quarter-deck. His first aid duties, he realises, are about to become ever more onerous. The prevalent air of suffering is aggravated by the repeated screams of one individual, a high-pitched, piercing wail. Nearby, the lieutenant observes the efforts of a first aid team who try to treat a severely-wounded seaman. In a bizarre moment the seaman strikes out with his fists before, in a sudden act of insanity, he attempts to rip off his own bandages. The first aid men use forcible restraint before they make renewed efforts to apply tourniquets.

In another terrible scene, the lieutenant glimpses first aiders who strive to curb the flow of blood from a leg stump that thrashes wildly in the air. Such a challenge, he thinks, would test the best efforts of a fully-trained, fully-equipped surgical team. The cries of the victim, his frail and vulnerable state as he observes his own injuries, add to a widespread sense of inadequacy. The man's trauma and his transparent confusion heighten his attendants' anxiety as they struggle to apply treatment. The first aid teams, though, face a fine balance: forthcoming surgery will dictate the cautious use of pain-killing drugs, but a patient in excessive pain may enter a deep and fatal shock.

While the rescue activities proceed, the lieutenant overhears conversations about the ship's popular master-at-arms, Mr Luddington, who was seen to enter the hangar deck. A large and strong man, as master-at-arms he evidently felt duty-bound to assist rescue parties in the hangar area. Now, however, he has been found dead, his body badly burned. In a further report, the lieutenant hears that just three have survived the blast in the wardroom (thankfully, these have included his pilot for the attack last year against the Italian Fleet at Taranto, Lieutenant Torrens-Spence). Other reports indicate that a headless corpse, still upright in a scorched wardroom armchair and still clutching an open copy of *The Times*, turned out to be that of the Royal Air Force liaison officer.

"Alfie!" Lieutenant Sutton hears a faint cry from behind. He turns around. "Over here, Alfie." He spots a man laid on his side, part of his backbone exposed.

"Alfie!" The man's husky voice is hard to make out so the lieutenant leans towards him.

"Who...?" the lieutenant hesitates as he begins to recognise the distorted features of Lieutenant Gregory, a Fulmar fighter pilot. "My dear chap..." he attempts to soothe his colleague's obvious distress.

"Don't worry about..." the fighter pilot's voice trails away.

"Hang on, old fellow. I'll see what can be done." Lieutenant Sutton, however, vacillates as he recognises that his capabilities at injury assessment, at correct and effective treatment, have reached their limits. When he gazes in perplexed consternation at Lieutenant Gregory, the latter detects this and hisses through clenched teeth:

"Don't worry about me, Alfie...I'm a gonner. You can't help me. Find another..."

Just at this moment, Lieutenant Sutton spots Padre Henry Lloyd who has left his position on the bridge in order to assist with first aid duties. As the padre looks around, the lieutenant waves him across. The padre dashes to the scene and the two grimly inspect their patient. The padre feels inside his medical pack, then kneels down to prepare a large injection of morphine. When this is applied, Lieutenant Sutton is moved by the priest's calm, kindly manner, and by his words of comfort to his patient. Later, Alfie will feel haunted by the poignancy of this moment. The sequel, however, will be equally heartbreaking. The fighter pilot, when repositioned by harassed stretcher-bearers, will be mishandled and the instant of his death will be signified by a sharp crack when his backbone snaps.

Meanwhile, as Major Enneccerus and his formations of Ju 87Bs withdraw from their attack, personnel on the *Illustrious* squint their eyes to observe the Stukas disappear in a northerly direction. Anti-aircraft defences fall silent; the enemy's initial onslaught has ended and crew members can breathe temporary sighs of relief. The men, however, know that they should brace themselves for further attacks. This, they realise, will be just a matter of time. Any pause in proceedings is bound to be short-lived.

15

Malta Waits

If Miss Sybil Dobbie feels a sense of guilt, this is probably unwarranted. Maybe from time to time, as she sits patiently by the tennis court to await the arrival of other players, the realisation of her privileged position will strike her. Then again, maybe such aspirations are a little too fanciful. Nonetheless, the pleasing glimpses of her grand surroundings, her appreciation of the beneficial Mediterranean climate, the thoughts of her present circumstances – so distant from those of her friends at home – all combine, perhaps, to prompt occasional twinges of conscience... although, on due reflection, this is a favoured lifestyle to which, no doubt, she has become happily accustomed.

The game of tennis which she is about to enjoy will be in the grounds of Malta's Palace of Saint Anton. Today's match will be a light-hearted affair with her father (who is the island's governor), his *aide-de-camp*, and another member of his staff.

As she waits, Miss Dobbie reflects that despite the afternoon's mid-winter chill, the brightness of the January day somehow accentuates the grandeur of the palace, especially the white brilliance of its elaborate exterior. Situated in the heart of the island, the palace and its gardens occupy coveted space within Malta's small surface area of just ninety-five square miles, about one sixth the size of Greater London. Its enigmatic contrasts – the hilly south-eastern region separated from the flatter north-west area by the Great Fault – is enhanced by the inhabitants' friendly attitudes and their stoical outlooks. Perhaps this can be attributed (in part, at least) to the island's years as a fortress colony, the influence through the centuries of the influx of various groups of immigrant mercenaries, workers and even slaves.

Miss Dobbie glances down to check her tennis racquet. When she looks up again, she frowns. Her father must have been held up. The Palace of

Saint Anton stands proudly, and Miss Dobbie values the sense of history that complements the building with its fine grounds. She knows how much her father appreciates the aura of quiet distinction that befits his official residence with its unusual gardens. However the exotic nature of these gardens is inconsistent with the island's general flora and fauna: Malta's stony karst landscape means that vegetables, fruit, and most other forms of vegetation are hard to cultivate. This merely adds to the island's present difficulties with shortages of just about everything.

Her father, however, General Sir William Dobbie, is an energetic governor. A former British army sapper, he has mustered the support of the Maltese population, bolstered their morale and has persuaded them to make the most of limited resources. When promoted from his post as acting governor to become the island's governor and commander-in-chief, he had proved how he was a man of strong religious faith.

On 10th June last year, the day when Mussolini had declared war on Britain and one of the days when the British Expeditionary Force had been in the process of desperate evacuation from the beaches of Dunkirk, General Dobbie had delivered a broadcast to the people of Malta. He had called upon the populace to show faith and fortitude similar to his own, and his assumption that the religiously-minded Maltese would react positively had been correct.

The staunchly Roman Catholic population, whose large numbers of churches include one that was capable of accommodating a congregation of many thousands of worshippers (the church of Saint Maria Assunta in the village of Mosta), had warmed to the new governor even though his beliefs were at the opposite end of the religious spectrum to their own. The Maltese people had shown due respect for the governor's sincerity of religious conviction as a Seventh-Day Adventist.

In the distance, Miss Dobbie thinks that she can make out her father's voice. She hears other voices, too, a number of men are talking. Her father is fortunate to have the support of dedicated individuals, especially the likes of Air Commodore Maynard and Vice-Admiral Wilbraham Ford, his senior assistants, although her father is guided by civil servants and sometimes she wonders if the fond focus on bureaucratic minutiae might lead to a blurring of overview. Nonetheless the governor and his team have done stalwart work as they set about husbanding the island's resources. They have organised troop training, established effective anti-aircraft cover, and instituted other necessary defence arrangements.

Although her father's plans for conscription of able-bodied men were regarded without enthusiasm by some of the islanders, Miss Dobbie believes that the population as a whole must have recognised, surely, the imperative need for measures to deal with the enemy and his despicable activities.

Many of Malta's present-day problems have been caused by lack of foresight. The strained British defence budget of the late 1930s reflected the island's low priority and as a result Malta's defences now proved woefully inadequate. The island's garrison apparently comprised just a few battalions and there is a lack of the fighter aircraft needed so urgently to counter those hateful bombers of the Italian Regia Aeronautica. At least, she thinks, efforts have been made to rectify the situation, although she was intrigued, appalled even, by the story her father had told her about last November's attempts to fly some Hurricane fighter aircraft to the island. Evidently, a dozen of these machines had been launched from a Royal Navy ship, then led towards Malta by a decorated Battle of Britain veteran. It appears, however, that someone had miscalculated the notoriously nefarious Mediterranean winds, and as the flight had progressed, the poor fighter pilots were subjected to a creeping realisation that, in all probability, they would run out of fuel before Malta was reached.

One of the Hurricanes in the leading section of fighters had insufficient fuel to reach Malta and the machine had been forced, therefore, to ditch in the sea nearly fifty miles short of its destination. Other aircraft had made it to one of the island's aerodromes, but only just: it appeared that fuel margins were so tight that the engine of one of the Hurricanes had cut out before the machine even reached the end of the runway.

Her father had then told her that a sub-flight of fighters had fared even worse. Apparently, the navigator in a Skua-lead aircraft had got hopelessly lost and the fighters he was supposed to lead to safety had fallen away one by one as their fuel exhausted. Although the Skua itself made it to an island, it was the wrong one! Italian anti-aircraft flak had greeted the Skua when it crossed the coast of Sicily and caused it to crash-land. When this news reached him, the governor was as devastated as Admiral Somerville, the man in charge of the operation.

A slight furore causes Miss Dobbie to stand up and gaze in the direction of the palace. She concludes, however, that the matter is of little consequence. The voluble tones of an excited maid seem indecipherable in any case. The Maltese are no less inclined to hot-blooded excitement than other Mediterranean folk, and the islanders' present living conditions hardly helped to soothe tempers.

The island benefits from subterranean sources of water, otherwise local people are forced to depend on regular re-supply by the so-called WS ('Winston Special') convoys. Everything shipped to Malta is rapidly consumed and the governor and his staff are faced with constant logistical problems. Like the spades, diamonds, clubs and hearts in some well-thumbed packed of cards shuffled by a poker player, these men have to juggle the requirements of food, fuel, medical stores, guns, ammunition, vehicles, reinforcements, all the essentials needed to sustain life in the island's war-torn environment.

From time to time she wonders about her reactions to things, about her unstated awareness of her own vulnerability, that of her family. Malta's isolation could produce a sense of personal loneliness. Naturally she is not the only one to feel like this, and that the island's reputation as Melita (the 'honeyed one') is well deserved in a peacetime situation. She has greater reason to be thankful than most, and she should try to be seen to set a good example of cheerful determination.

"Sorry we're late, Sybil." At last Miss Dobbie can spot her father as he and the others hasten towards the tennis court. A short warm-up session ensues before the game is under way.

"Love fifteen. Well played." The governor waves cheerily as he prepares himself for the next serve.

"Love thirty." Miss Dobbie glares at her tennis racquet.

"Fifteen thirty."

"Fifteen forty." Once more, Miss Dobbie gazes gloomily at the strings of her tennis racquet. "Sorry!" she says. She prepares for the next shot but then stops quite suddenly, her racquet in mid-air. She angles her head as she lowers her racket but she says nothing at first.

"Sybil? Are you all right?"

"So sorry…it's just that…"

"Well?"

"Can you not hear it?"

"Hear what?"

"Listen!"

"I can't hear anything unusual."

"Yes, there's something peculiar going on…listen carefully…listen to that noise in the background."

"I can hear it now. The sound of distant guns."

"What can it be?"

"I'm not exactly sure," says the governor grimly. "But I think we'd better find out." His curt nod, his worried look, bring the game of tennis to an abrupt end.

16

Ongoing Battle

As Major Enneccerus leads his formations of Ju 87 Stukas due north towards their bases in Sicily, shortage of fuel forces the Fulmar fighters of HMS *Illustrious* to break off pursuit. Lieutenant Sutton (who has been too preoccupied to know about the activities of these Fulmars) carries on with first aid duties on the quarter-deck. At present, the lieutenant remains unaware of the disruption caused to the Stukas and to the precision of their final attacks. Several Stukas were forced to release their bombs prematurely and five enemy machines have been shot down. Despite such interference, however, the Luftwaffe action will be described later by the *Illustrious*'s captain as…'severe, brilliantly executed, and pressed home with the utmost skill and determination'.

The Swordfish pilot of 815 Squadron, whose earlier attempts to land on the carrier were interrupted by the Stukas, described the scene from an airborne perspective:

'In a lull between desperate turns, I managed a quick look upwards to see where all the Stukas were coming from. I saw several clusters in tight formation, circling very high in the sky, like wasps awaiting their turn to dive on a pot of jam. I saw them peeling off, one by one; tiny objects, their wings glinting in the sun. They rolled away from the formation slowly – almost casually – as though they were taking part in some air display and had all the time in the world. As each silvery dot sped downwards, it grew bigger with every fraction of a second, and its dive became steeper until it was a huge blob of an aeroplane with a swastika on its side, diving vertically through the ship's barrage.

'Their flying was very skilled and they pressed home their attacks with no thought for their own safety…I saw dozens of men rushing about the flight deck with hoses. Around them, the length and breadth of deck was a mass of steam. The heat from the hangar below turned water into vapour as soon as it touched the hot steel beneath their scorched feet.'

While they watch the Stukas head north, the ship's aircrew must rue the frustration of their position. Their once-proud carrier is now a smoking wreck, reduced in a matter of minutes from potent threat to impotent liability. The flight deck is unusable and aircraft will have to head south in order to refuel and rearm at airfields in Malta before returning to defend the ship.

Later, Lieutenant Sutton will learn details of the initial enemy assault. The first bomb struck at 1238 hours (around the time he approached the hangar *en route* to the bridge) but did not enter the hangar itself. That bomb hit the loading platform of the forward pom-pom gun, wounded two of the gun's crew, penetrated the ship's side, and exploded on impact with the sea. The next bomb struck the armoured plating on the ship's bow, passed through the flight deck, then detonated in the paint-store. A third bomb, armed with an impact fuse, missed the carrier's island by less than two feet before falling on the number two starboard pom-pom gun and killing all of the crew.

The gun was dismounted by the explosion which caused steel splinters to strike the nearby number one pom-pom crew. The next bomb, a 500-kilogram armour-piercing projectile, crashed through the carrier's after lift and exploded inside the hangar. This blast, at 1240 hours, knocked Lieutenant Sutton off his feet, hurled him through two water-tight door openings and deposited him in the officers' accommodation area.

While damage-control parties rushed to the scene, fire screens were lowered. The hangar fires were tackled swiftly and the situation was almost under control when another bomb penetrated the wreckage of the after lift. The lift's distorted angle deflected the bomb into the hangar where it blew up. The steel fire screens disintegrated causing shards of red-hot metal to ricochet through the hangar. A few seconds later, another bomb exploded under the ship's bow. Blast damage arched the forward lift which exacerbated the effect of wind fanning the fires.

At this point, the last group of Stukas commenced their dives. However, Fulmar fighters by then had gained sufficient altitude to harass the Stukas, although the latter still managed to drop one bomb on the flight deck, some six metres forward of the after lift. The stressed flight deck fractured; the bomb entered the hangar and exploded on the ammunition conveyor. The carrier's electrical power failed and when electric pumps stopped, fire parties lost the means to control fires. The *Illustrious* then started to slow; the great ship lay askew the line of the Mediterranean Fleet as smoke and giant flickers of flame gradually engulfed her.

At length, with the restoration of electrical power, fire fighting could resume. Just now, as fire control and other efforts persist, the carrier's senior officers try to assess the situation. The ship is still ninety nautical miles from Malta, she has developed a list to starboard, and steams in a circle. The international signal that she is not under command has been raised, but this is obscured by steam and smoke. Various fires still burn fiercely.

The carrier's electrically-controlled steam steering system is inoperative and so far three attempts to complete the circuitry have failed. On the plus side, the steam turbines are still serviceable and the ship is capable of seventeen knots. When, at last, the carrier's rudder is induced amidships, the captain can make use of the carrier's multiple screws to steer the ship. As the *Illustrious* maintains a steady course for Malta, crew morale rises when her speed creeps up to a satisfactory twenty-one knots.

Meanwhile, Lieutenant Sutton continues with rescue duties on the ship's quarter-deck. As further casualties are brought to the area, some are evacuated to the ship's main sick bay, fortunately still functional. First aid parties have to carry heavily-laden stretchers through flame-swept after ladders, across the hot and hazardous flight deck, then down the ship's forward ladders to the sick bay.

Attempts to prioritise the wounded are made, but the lieutenant finds these and other rescue efforts hampered by haphazard distractions: a rescuer's sudden glimpse of his own blood-soaked hands; eerie silences broken by abrupt shrieks; the glazed looks of the severely shocked; the cries of the wounded mingle with the moans of the dying. If rescuers start to flag, individuals are encouraged by colleagues who realise that if the ship and her crew are to be saved, rescue efforts must be unstinting. Crewmen who witness personal acts of courage and leadership are infused with renewed spirit. Brute force and wholehearted energy have to act as a drug for other feelings.

Some twenty minutes after Major Enneccerus and his Stukas flew away due north, the *Illustrious* receives warning of another possible attack. Information is flashed around the fleet that radar operators on HMS *Valiant* have picked up airborne echoes. By now, however, the Fulmar fighters have departed for Malta and Admiral Cunningham is without air cover. The admiral therefore orders his fleet to close on to the carrier and to stand by to throw up a barrage of fire. When enemy formations approach at 14,000 feet, the barrage is delivered with due vigour. Seven SM 79 aircraft of the Regia Aeronautica attempt to drop bombs, but the Italians apparently lack the aggression of their Luftwaffe allies: the bombs are dropped wide, and the aircraft withdraw.

Unfortunately, any sense of relief on board the *Illustrious* is short-lived. The carrier's rudder starts to give further trouble and the ship enters a series of erratic turns which endanger nearby escorts. Engineering staff strive for some thirty minutes to remedy the fault. By 1400 hours they manage to steady the *Illustrious* on a course for Malta, although her speed has to be reduced to fifteen knots. Captain Boyd knows that if his ship is to survive, the carrier must reach Malta with minimum delay. He therefore orders his boiler-room staff to maintain steam 'whatever the cost'.

The cost, however, seems to mount. As fires rage in the hangar deck, local temperatures in the boiler room below rise to the point where bulkheads start to glow, and staff begin to faint. Huge ventilator fans draw toxic fumes and smoke into the boiler room where personnel have to hold wet rags to faces and form chains to report water pressures and levels from gauges which are barely visible. Men who fight asphyxiation and overheating are forced to drink unsavoury water from the feed pumps.

In the hangar deck above, fire-control teams continue to cope with explosions from burning ammunition, petroleum and aircraft. The intense heat has begun to weld steel pipes and even melt bronze valves. The teams use water, foamite and asbestos but nothing seems to quench the fires which now threaten the carrier's main magazine and her upper fuel tanks.

On the quarter-deck, Lieutenant Sutton surveys lines of filthy, oil-soaked casualties, some who sit upright, others who lay sprawled. He observes strong sailors reduced to pitiful culprits with blackened faces that stare blankly at the sky, men who crouch to control violent shivers, individuals who glance at the limbless, lifeless forms of one-time colleagues. The division between the living and the dead becomes increasingly blurred. A petty officer, his cheeks and temples blistered by burns, tries to rouse a friend: "Bert? Is that you over there, Bert?" The padre's voice can be heard while he tends to a Catholic shipmate…"*Requiem aeternam dona eis, Domine; et lux perpetua luceat eis; Te decet hymnus, Deus, in Sion, et tibi reddetur votum in Jerusalem…*"

By 1500 hours, just as the *Illustrious*'s prospects seem at their bleakest, the ship's senior engineering officer makes a crucial discovery. A leaky oil line to the steering gear has been fuelling the fire. He advises the captain to suspend the steam steering system and fire fighters finally start to regain control. The ship's progression to Malta improves. The carrier's speed creeps up towards eighteen knots as a straight course to the island is held.

At this stage, Lieutenant Sutton attempts to coax an injured rating out of a potentially fatal desire to drift into sleep. The young rating – a cheerful Cockney in normal times – seems to have given up hope. The lieutenant, as he urges the other to stay awake, tries to recall Cockney jokes, expressions, rhyming slang: "'Call yourself a true Cockney? Born and bred within earshot of Bow Bells? Come on now lad! Stay awake…" The rating's mumbled replies are hard to discern. The lieutenant tries again: "Come on, lad…keep going…look at me!"

The rating struggles to look up. As he does so, he half turns to observe the sky. At that moment, both men become aware of the racket of aircraft aloft. All eyes squint upwards as anti-aircraft guns – those that remain serviceable – open up again. Before long, when a particular howl is heard above the roar of the pom-poms, the implication is clear. The Stukas are back.

17

Absent Friends

Some fifteen Stukas, escorted by five Messerschmitt Me 110s, the machines under orders to complete the mission 'Illustrious *mussen sinken*', have taken advantage of the smoke screen behind the *Illustrious* to approach the carrier from astern. By now, however, with the time at around 1600 hours, the carrier's Fulmars have returned from Malta. The fighters manage to disrupt the attackers apart from one Stuka that breaks through to deliver a 500-kilogram bomb on the flight deck. The bomb lands within feet of the after lift well, bursts through the flight deck, and blows up inside a temporary sick-bay. In the resultant fireball, some thirty men are incinerated.

By 1730 hours, exhausted fire-fighters and damage-control parties send a message to the captain: the pumps are burnt out; the fires are out of control; permission is sought to flood the magazines. Captain Boyd, however, deems that such an act would be akin to surrender. He confirms that fire-fighting efforts must persist. As crewmen carry on with the struggle, those who work below the ship's waterline decide to undo their boot laces in order to expedite escape if 'abandon ship' is piped. These men know they would stand little chance if the magazines or the aviation fuel tanks were to blow up. One man, a stoker, comes across a war correspondent who, rather than go to the top for his story, asks to join the ratings in the stoke-hold. "Now you'll find out what fear really is," says the stoker.

As evening draws on, the captain is warned that further enemy attack is imminent. Italian SM 79s armed with torpedoes appear, but the half-dozen or so enemy machines are driven off by the ship's remaining operational guns and by fire from her close escorts. This proves to be the enemy's last action of the day. By 2145 hours, when nightfall conveniently conceals the carrier from hostile aircraft, she is met by tugs from the dockyard.

On the horizon, the light of a rising moon reveals the agreeable silhouette of land. Crew members strain to glimpse the low outline of the island of Malta. The men breathe silent sighs of relief when they realise that assistance at last is at hand, all has not been lost, and the respite of night – the refuge of Malta – will reward the day's fearsome battles.

By now, the free-surface effect of the fire-fighters' water has exacerbated the ship's lean. As the heavily-listing carrier is directed towards Parlatorio Wharf, Lieutenant Sutton is ordered to assume the duties of fo'c's'le officer (the officer normally assigned to the task remains too heavily involved with damage control). The *Illustrious* is edged alongside the wharf observed by large crowds who, having heard of the carrier's plight, have gathered to witness the great ship's arrival. A band has been organised and the crowds are entertained by jaunty music which, bizarrely, includes the tune of 'Roll out the Barrel'.

Naval headquarters at Malta and the island's admirable governor, whose game of tennis was interrupted by distant gunfire as the *Illustrious* was attacked, have rallied all possible aid to meet the carrier's requirements. Lines of ambulances wait by the wharf to take the injured to hospitals where medical teams stand by.

A witness to events would write later: '…they were needed. Lots and lots of men, mostly horribly burnt, were hurried in, and all that night and most of the next day the fight for their lives went on.' While the injured are tended, Lieutenant Sutton and other aircrew colleagues are taken to the air base at Hal Far where they will spend the next few nights. The men, however, will find their much-needed rest disturbed by tormented dreams.

On Saturday, 11th January 1941, scores of Maltese dockyard workers descend on the stricken carrier. The workers aim to make the ship seaworthy as rapidly as possible in order to facilitate her escape to Alexandria. Meanwhile, the ship's company is mustered by divisions for roll calls. While men stand forlornly on the damaged flight deck, if a name is called out and no-one answers, a chief petty officer will pause before asking if anyone has any information about that person. At length, grim statistics reveal that eighty-three officers and men have been killed, sixty critically injured, and forty less seriously wounded. Each survivor is given a telegram form and instructed to send a brief message to his next of kin. For security reasons, these messages have to be restricted to: 'I am all right, do not worry.' Soon, the story of the bombing will become headline news at home.

Lieutenant Sutton is dismayed to learn that the victims have included several of his aircrew colleagues, men who had survived the Taranto attack. He hears that young Sub-lieutenant Mardel-Ferreira RNVR has been killed, and that Sub-lieutenant Wray has been fatally wounded (he will die in hospital in Malta, with Captain Boyd at his bedside). Sub-lieutenant Perkins RNVR, who was knocked unconscious in the wardroom blast, is thought to have drowned in fire-fighters' water. Lieutenant Clifford, who was badly wounded by shrapnel, disappeared before he could be helped (he was believed to have been blown over the ship's side by one of the later bomb blasts, but his body will never be found).

In attempts to recover personal belongings, crew members will visit the carrier. Later, one pilot will write about his experience:

'Before leaving the ship I had a good look round. The sight which met my eyes was 100 percent worse than anything I had imagined. She had been such a beautiful ship inside, with quiet passages and neat cabins, nicely furnished...I found my cabin, eventually, after a nightmare search which still features in my dreams if I have a bad night. It had been completely filled with oily water right up to the deck-head and nothing remained. What was left of my clothing was unrecognisable but I found my little portable typewriter, its keyboard grinning at me with an obscene grimace; some trick of blast had folded it in two, like a sandwich...

'The hangar had always been the showpiece of the ship and the squadrons had always vied with each other to keep it spotless. Now it was no longer there. There was no trace of its deck, just a gaping void surrounded by grey tangled metal and the ship's sides visible to some fifty or sixty feet. Wherever one looked there were the signs of violent death in an open space of twisted disorder. I took one fearful look and fled.'

Lieutenant Sutton, whose own efforts to find personal belongings prove equally fruitless, decides to visit injured shipmates in hospital. In the hospital ward, where the mood is eerily subdued, he walks slowly past lines of beds. At one point he is called across by a rating:

"I want to thank you, sir."

"Thank me?"

"Yes, sir." The young man's eyes brim with emotion. "The doctors say that my hands have been saved and that this is largely due to the efficiency of my first aid treatment. I recognise you, sir, as the officer who applied the treatment and I just wanted to say a big 'thank you'."

The lieutenant tries to remain cheerful as he offers words of consolation. When, eventually, he moves to another part of the ward, he feels sickened by the sights that surround him. He glimpses haunted faces that lack eyebrows, ears, lips, even chins; the faces seem to present a living caricature of individual experience. He sees a junior nurse, no more than twenty years of age, bite her lip and fight back tears as she emerges from behind hastily-erected screens. She wrings her small hands in a gesture of dazed disbelief.

Behind the screens, medical staff communicate in low, anguished tones as they struggle to apply treatment to a patient's severe burns. The patient, meantime, lets out a series of low moans punctuated by hoarse screams. When he walks towards the junior nurse, the lieutenant catches her eye and tries to comfort her. As they pass, she turns her pale face to the heavens.

In another scene, a harassed medical officer and nursing sister check a young rating, his cheeks and forehead covered in raw, bluish-violet blisters. The young man's eyes ooze, as if afflicted by a case of severe conjunctivitis; his body stiffens when the nursing sister tries to apply a prepared solution to clean his eyes. At one stage, the weary medical officer grows impatient: "Keep still," he orders the rating. The lieutenant glances down as he continues along the ward. At least, he thinks, men seem to take some comfort in the knowledge of shared suffering. When he nears one bed, he hears his name called out.

"Alfie! Is that you?" He checks his pace then walks across to where a heavily-bandaged figure lies prone in bed. "I'm Sam," says the figure. In the subsequent conversation, expressions of encouragement help to boost the morale of Lieutenant Sam Morford, although the severity of his wounds mean that he will never fly again as aircrew.

Meanwhile, as the Maltese dockyard workers carry out repair work, divers go down to inspect the carrier below her waterline. The temporary wooden plugs inserted by the ship's damage-control teams are removed, metal is welded over the holes. Work on the flight deck and aircraft lifts is deemed non-essential, but workmen concentrate on repairs to the damaged steering gear. The once-familiar roar of aircraft engines is replaced by the clatter of pumps and generators, welding and acetylene torches, as the ship disappears under prodigious arrangements of scaffolding, ladders, and tarpaulin. Fortunately, dull and overcast weather conditions offer respite from the Luftwaffe's expected return.

However, on Monday, 13th January 1941, the weather improves. This day coincides with the arrival in Sicily of Major Paul-Werner Hozzel (described as 'swarthy, good looking, with unwavering eyes') who later will give the following account:

'German Supreme Command ordered, in the first few days of January 1941, Stuka Geschwader 3 from France to Sicily, to the Italian air station Trapani, situated at the north-west corner of the island. This geschwader was composed of two gruppen (wings), 1 Stuka 1 and 1

Stuka 2…At that time I was commander one of the 1 Stuka 1 peace-station, Insterburg in East Prussia…

'I flew down to Trapani and landed on 13th January 1941. Immediately after landing, I was told by my friend Major Enneccerus, commander two 1 Stuka 2, that the geschwader made an attack on 10th January against a big convoy protected by the aircraft carrier *Illustrious*. As observed during attack, *Illustrious*…went lop-sided and could not move.

'We then suffered with bad weather which lasted for several days… and conditions were still awful when Supreme Commander of the Luftwaffe (Field-Marshal Göring) ordered us to sink *Illustrious* at the quays of La Valetta…

'Because of this we lost our best crews…when I rose in the morning I knew with certainty that by sinking sun some five or six crews would have gone. One day, after the last mission, the leader of my second squadron, who was a very hard chap, could not report to me for his tears. He was the sole remaining member of his squadron; he had lost all his men.

'From then we got new, strict, orders to do our best to sink this ship once and for all. So we went to Catania air station and there loaded 1,000-kilogram bombs. With these bombs we needed about one-and-a-half hours to reach an altitude of 3,000 metres. We succeeded in dropping four on the deck of the *Illustrious*, but she still did not sink because our bombs were not able to penetrate the armoured decks below and because of numerous bulkheads.'

When the air-raid sirens are sounded in Valetta, the *Illustrious*'s crews hasten to uncover the ship's guns. In the meantime, the dockyard workers dash from their places of work to shelter in the caves of nearby Senglea. Luftwaffe Stuka Geschwader strikes create havoc as 'plane after plane drops like a hawk to its prey'. Observers watch the machines descend so low over Grand harbour that the aircraft fly beneath the level of the Maltese-manned gun emplacements.

One Bofors battery commander, Lieutenant Micallef Trigona (a Maltese territorial officer), becomes so infuriated by the cool waves and grins of passing Stuka pilots that he orders the removal of safety railings. At the Stukas' next pass, Lieutenant Trigona could be seen by his Bofors gun, now at a suitably depressed angle, his angled right arm thumped by his left hand in a gesture of unmistakable Latin origin.

On Thursday, 16th January 1941, the Luftwaffe raids reach new peaks. The *Illustrious* is attacked by over forty Stukas, backed by seventeen Ju 88s, ten Messerschmitt Me 110s, ten Fiat CR 42 fighters and some Macchi

200s. In a whirlwind of scaffolding, ladders and tarpaulin, the carrier suffers a hit and surrounding dock areas are left in a chaos of flame and devastation.

The initial attack lasts for several minutes after which the bombers retreat. Further waves appear during the day, and although the *Illustrious* herself avoids another hit, by nightfall the cargo-liner *Essex* has been struck leaving sixteen of her crew dead and twenty-three wounded. The engine room of the *Essex* has taken the force of the blast; her officers reckon that if the cargo of 4,000 tons of ammunition had been hit, the resultant explosion would have destroyed the *Illustrious* and a large part of Valetta. The Maltese dockers, badly shaken by such a narrow escape, threaten to discontinue work. The governor therefore orders that soldiers and airmen should be sent to assist with the unloading of the *Essex*.

The *Illustrious*'s engineering commander, Lieutenant-Commander 'Pincher' Martin, and his men work with unremitting dedication to repair the new damage caused (he will be awarded a Distinguished Service Cross). He reports to the captain that the engines remain in a satisfactory condition and that he reckons they will be able to make the ship seaworthy in a few days.

The captain leaves a skeleton crew on board, but he evacuates the bulk of his men to the air base at Hal Far. In attempts to neutralise the British fighter effort, the Luftwaffe decide to bomb Hal Far but their losses, as recorded by Major Hozzel, rise to unsustainable levels. The Luftwaffe's raids of 16th January result in the estimated destruction of some ten of their aircraft without corresponding British loss. German losses would be even greater in a raid of three days later.

In an interlude between enemy assaults, a navy wife will visit the *Illustrious*. She would recall later how…

'…officers and men came in and out of the tunnel (the dockyard air raid shelter) and the surgery. Their faces looked lined and grimy. They were dressed in old boiler overalls, in grey flannel trousers and sweaters, any odd garment they had managed to save from the wrecks of the cabins. The surgeon of the ship had done wonderful work in the battle at sea. He was pale, and his face was very, very sad. It was the first time I had ever been on board a wounded ship. When I saw the great torn decks, the aching chasm that reached into her bowels, the little sick bay that had known such horror, I felt almost as near to tears as when I talked with her tired seamen.'

The *Illustrious* spends two weeks in Malta during which period most of her crew, for security reasons, would have little idea about the progress of repairs. However, on the afternoon of 23rd January 1941, the crewmen will be ordered to return to ship. That evening, under the cover of nightfall, the darkened ship slips secretly out of harbour. General Dobbie, at the time in session with the Council of Malta, hears someone call out: "She's off – and safe."

The *Illustrious* steams at twenty-six knots towards Alexandria in Egypt which she reaches safely in three days. The next stage of her journey would be to the USA to receive a complete refit at Norfolk, Virginia. Special curtains will replace the hangar's metal fire screens; never again will these be used on British aircraft carriers. In his report, Captain Boyd will pay tribute to 'the sound construction of the ship which enabled her to withstand such heavy punishment'. Awards for what will become known as the '*Illustrious* Blitz' will include a Distinguished Service Order for the ship's senior doctor, Surgeon-Commander Keevil, and crew members' shouts of delight will greet the news of a most unusual but well-deserved award: a Distinguished Service Order for the ship's padre, the Reverend Henry Lloyd.

Many months later, on 29th November 1941, HMS *Illustrious* will be re-commissioned. In 1954 she will be paid off before being scrapped at Faslane on 3rd November 1956.

Some days before the carrier's clandestine departure from Malta, Lieutenant Sutton and his colleagues are dispersed from Hal Far. The night before leaving by cruiser for Alexandria, a group of the aircrew meet in the officers' mess at Hal Far. The group discuss the news – just received – that amongst those mentioned in the captain's record, Lieutenant Sutton has been cited for gallantry. The assembled officers raise their glasses to congratulate their colleague.

"Well done, Alfie."

"Thank you." The lieutenant bows his head in acknowledgement, then raises his glass again. "To absent friends," he says.

"To absent friends," comes the reply, followed by a moment or two of silence. During the quiet spell, when the men become absorbed in thought, the lieutenant sees some look down, others glance upwards at the mess ceiling, a few stare blankly at their hands. All seem anxious to avoid the betrayal of private thoughts. The lieutenant, though, reckons that the officers' looks and their sober expressions alone provide sufficient comment. For these are men, he thinks, whose habit of understatement is synonymous with the quiet courage that belies the mighty significance of their achievements.

Top left: A W F Sutton at
Christ's Hospital School.

Top right: A W F Sutton as a
cadet at HMS *Erebus*, 1930.

Middle: Swordfish aircraft
launches from HMS
Glorious, 1938.

Bottom: HMS *Repulse*.

Top left: Lieutenant A W F Sutton, 1935.

Top right: Swordfish aircraft after landing on HMS *Glorious*, 1938.

Middle: Swordfish aircraft ranged on the deck of HMS *Glorious*, 1938.

Bottom left: Swordfish on the deck of HMS *Illustrious*.

Bottom right: Lieutenant and Mrs Sutton, married at Buckfast Abbey, January 1940.

By the KING'S Order the name of
Lieutenant Alan William Frank Sutton, R.N.

was published in the London Gazette on
1 January, 1941,
as mentioned in a Despatch for distinguished service.
I am charged to record
His Majesty's high appreciation.

First Lord of the Admiralty

A.F.O. 101/41.
New Year's Honours List - London Gazette Supplement of 1st January 1941

The King has been graciously pleased to give orders for
Appointments to the Distinguished Service Order, and to approve
Awards as shown below, for outstanding zeal, patience and
cheerfulness, and for never failing to set an example of
wholehearted devotion to duty, without which the high tradition
of the Royal Navy could not have been upheld:-

Mention in Despatches
Lieutenant Alan William Frank Sutton, Royal Navy, H.M.S.
"Illustrious".

The Lords Commissioners of the Admiralty
hereby certify that
by the KING'S order the name of
Lieutenant Alan William Frank Sutton, R.N.
H. M. S. Illustrious
was published in the London Gazette on
14 January, 1941.
as mentioned in Despatches for good service
of which His Majesty's high appreciation
is thus recorded.

A.F.O. 305/41.
Honours and Awards - London Gazette Supplement of 14th January 1941

The King has been graciously pleased to give orders for
the following Appointments to the Distinguished Service Order, and
to approve the following Awards:-

For courage, enterprise and devotion to duty in contact with
the enemy:
Mention in Despatches
Lieutenant Alan William Frank Sutton, Royal Navy, H.M.S.
"Illustrious

Top left: Lieutenant A W F Sutton Mentioned in
Despatches, 1 Jan 1941 and corresponding notice
detailing the award in the *London Gazette*.

Top right: Aerial port bow view of the aircraft
carrier HMS *Illustrious*.

Bottom left: Lieutenant A W F Sutton is Mentioned
in Despatches twice in two weeks. The *London
Gazette* again reports his decoration for good
service aboard the *Illustrious*.

Bottom right: Lieutenant 'Alfie' Sutton, 1940.

Top: Fairey Swordfish carrying an aerial torpedo.

Middle: Allied troops disembarking at Suda Bay (Alexander Turnbull Library)

Bottom: Fairey Fulmar approaching to land.

NO. C 68   17th February 1941

This is to certify that *Mr. A.J.W. Sutton*

has served as *Lieutenant. R.N.* in

"ILLUSTRIOUS" under my command from the

day of *June* 1940, to the *14th* day

of *January* 1941, during which period

he has conducted himself *to my entire satisfaction*
An expert observer and an able leader. He behaved
with gallantry during the air attacks on Jan 10th.

Denis W. Boyd   (Captain.
                                   (H.M.S. ILLUSTRIOUS

Top: Report by the captain of HMS *Illustrious*.

Middle left: General Freyberg VC, commanding officer of the British forces on Crete, gazes over the parapet of his dug-out in the direction of the German advance.

Middle right: German mountain troops prior to their transfer to Crete. (German Federal Archive).

Bottom: German parachutists over Crete.

NAVAL AWARDS

BATTLE OF CRETE

"GALLANTRY, FORTITUD[E] AND RESOLUTION"

The King has given orders for the f[ol]lowing appointments for gallantry, lead[er]ship, and skill during the Battle [of] Crete :—

C.B.

Rear-Admiral H. B. Rawlings, O.B.E.
Captain J. A, V. Morse, D.S.O., R.N.

The following appointments and awards also announced for outstanding gallantry, fo[rti]tude, and resolution during the Battle [of] Crete :—

BAR TO THE D.S.O.

Atg. Capt. C. H. Petrie, D.S.O., R.N., H.[M].S. Glengyle ; Cdr. W. G. A. Robson, D.S.O., D.S.C., R. H.M.S. Kandahar.

DISTINGUISHED SERVICE ORDER

Capt. S. H. T. Arliss, R.N. ; Capt. P. B. R. William-Powlett, R.N., H.M.S. Fiji ; Cdr. G. H. B[e] O.B.E., R.N. ; Cdr. A. St. C. Ford, R.N., H.M.S. [?] ling ; Cdr. H. A. King, R.N., H.M.S. Kashmir ; Cdr. H. F. Atkins, R.N., H.M.S. Orion ; Lieut.-Cdr. W. P[?] R.N., H.M.S. Carlisle.

BAR TO D.S.C.

Cdr. K. Michell, D.S.O., M.V.O., D.S.C., [?] (Retired) ; Lieut.-Cdr. I. G. Robertson, D.S.C., R. Lieut.-Cdr. P. Somerville, D.S.O., D.S.C., R. H.M.S. Kingston ; Lieut.-Cdr. J. I. Miller, D.S D.S.C., R.D., R.N.R. ; Lieut. I. F. D. Bush, D.S R.N. ; Lieut. A. W. F. Sutton, D.S.C., R.N. ; Te[mp.] Lieut. B. W. Waters, D.S.C., R.N.V.R.

DISTINGUISHED SERVICE CROSS

Cdr. C. Wauchope, R.N. ; Cdr. (E) G. McD. Wil[?] R.A.N.
Lieut.-Cdr. M. Alliston, R.N., H.M.S. Kandah[ar] Lieut.-Cdr. M. R. E. Faering, R.N. ; Lieut.-Cdr. J. Forman, R.N., H.M.S. Kingston ; Lieut.-Cdr. J. Hicks, R.N., H.M.S. Orion ; Lieut.-Cdr. G. Tal[?] Smith, R.N., H.M.A.S. Perth ; Lieut.-Cdr. G. Mor[?] R.N.R. (Retired) ; Lieut.-Cdr. M. J. Clark, R.A Surg.-Lieut.-Cdr. E. M. Tymms, R.A.N.V.R. ; H.M. Perth ; Lieut. C. R. Havergal, R.N., H.M.S. Kandah[ar] Lieut.-Cdr. (E) H. C. Hogger, R.N., H.M.S. Kiplin[?] Lieut. P. W. B. Ashmore, R.N., H.M.S. Kelly ; Lieut. R. A. Haig, R.N., H.M.S. Glenroy ; Li[eut.] D. H. F. Hetherington, R.N., H.M.S. Kimber[?] Lieut. I. L., T. Hogg, R.N., H.M.A.S. Napier ; L[ieut.] G. J. A. Lumsden, R.N., H.M.S. Phoebe ; Lieut. [?] Norton, R.N., H.M.S. Fiji ; Lieut. A. D. Robin, R. H.M.S. Kelly ; Lieut. L. M. Hinchcliffe, R.A H.M.A.S. Napier ; Temp. Lieut. J. E. Woodw[?] R.N.V.R. ; Surg.-Lieut. R. I. Bence, M.A., B. B.Ch., R.N.V.R. ; Surg.-Sub-Lieut. E. B. McDowall, M B.Ch., M.R.C.S., C.R.C.P., R.N.V.R. ; H.[M.S.] Nubian ; Surg.-Lieut. C. F. Harrington, R.A.N Lieut. (A) L. K. Keith, R.N. ; Temp. Lieut. (A) R. Ramsay, R.N.V.R. ; Lieut. (E) J. E. C. Ogg[?] R.N. ; Lieut. (E) W. J. Spendlow, R.N., H.[M.S.] Decoy ; Lieut. (Atg. Capt.) P. Beeman, R. Mar[?] H.M.S. Calcutta ; Temp. Pmr. Lieut. S. H. Th[?] R.N.V.R. ; Temp. Sub-Lieut. J. D. Thom, R.N[.V.R.] H.M.S. Glenroy ; Atg. Sub-Lieut. S. S. Brooks, [?] H.M.S. Fiji.
Mr. J. M. S. Lenton, Atg. Gnr. (T), R.N., H.[M.S.] Kandahar ; Mr. A. J. Brown, Gnr., R.A.N., H.M.S. Parramatta ; Mr. W. R. Hare, Wnt. Shipwright, R H.M.S. Orion ; Mr. H. C. Hill, Wnt. Mechani[c] R.A.N., H.M.A.S. Perth ; Mr. T. W. Pick, Wnt. Te[?] R.N. ; Skipper W. Stewart, R.N.R. ; Mid. J. [?] Thompson, R.N., H.M.S. Orion.

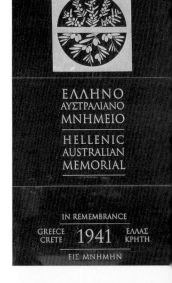

Top left: Fairey Fulmar in flight.

Top right: Lieutenant Sutton was later awarded the Bar to his DSC as reported here in *The Times*, 1942.

Middle: Captured German paratroopers under British guard.

Bottom left: More German paratroopers drop over Crete (German Federal Archive).

Bottom right: Greek memorial of the Battle of Crete.

Top: British wounded finally disembark at Alexandria after being evacuated.

Middle left: General Bernard Freyberg during the Battle of Cassino, 1944.

Middle right: A copy of the note left by German troops after the bombing of the prison and consequent escape of many inmates as mentioned in the text.

Bottom: The *London Gazette* details the awarding of Lieutenant A W F Sutton's Distinguished Service Cross for bravery displayed in the Battle of Taranto.

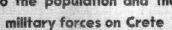

To the population and the military forces on Crete

It has been brought to the notice of the German Supreme Command that German soldiers who fell into the hands of the enemy on the island of Crete have been illtreated and even mutilated in a most infamous and inhuman manner.

As a punishment and reprisal therefore is announced as follows:

1) Whosoever commits such crimes against international laws on German prisoners of war will be punished in the manner of his own cruel action; no matter be he or she a man or a woman.

2) Localities near which such crimes have been perpetrated will be burned down. The population will be held responsible.

3) Beyond these measures further and sharper reprisals will be held in store.

The German Supreme Command

A.F.O. 2231/41.
Honours and Awards - London Gazette Supplement of 20th May 1941

In "London Gazette" Supplement No. 35018, of 20th December, 1940, it was announced that the King has been graciously pleased to give orders for the following Appointment to the Distinguished Service Order, and to approve the following Award, for outstanding courage and skill in a brilliant and wholly successful night attack by the Fleet Air Arm on the Italian Fleet at Taranto:

His Majesty has now been further graciously pleased to give orders for the following Appointments to the Distinguished Service Order, and to approve the following Awards for outstanding courage and skill in this action:

The Distinguished Service Cross
Lieutenant Alan William Frank Sutton, Royal Navy, H.M.S.
"Illustrious"

Captain Alan Sutton DSC & Bar, 1955.

PART TWO

Crete Conflict

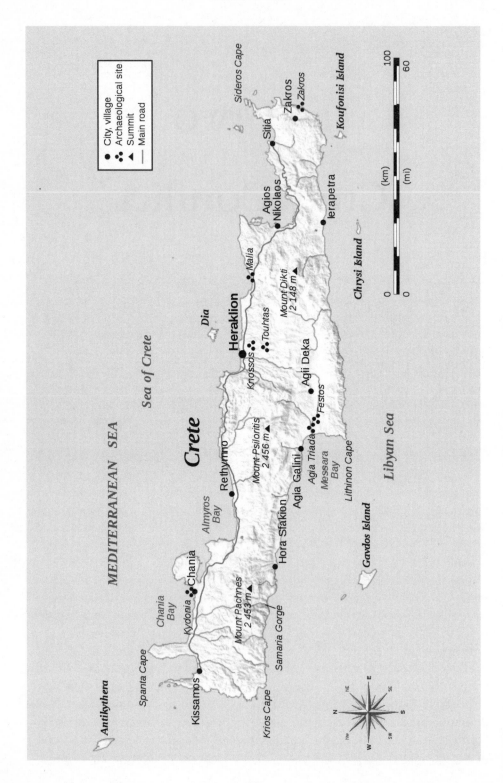

18

Dawn Chorus

Monday, 19th May 1941

He is awakened by the urgent chorus of birdsong.

The lieutenant's initial instincts (alarm…threat… danger) hardly are allayed when confusions of unlikely scent (wild thyme and olive wood – goat droppings – the sweet smell of orange blossom) waft sublimely into his tent. For some moments he lies still in his camp-bed trying to pick up latent sounds of danger within the birdsong. The aura of peril is real enough, and imminent, so no-one can afford to relax, although just now the birdsong appears to lack any form of unwelcome accompaniment.

As he listens, he ponders the natural world's indifference to the machinations of mankind; the new dawn proceeds regardless of himself and his own precarious situation. The heady atmosphere of his surroundings may heighten his sense of apprehension but soon he must rouse and then, as the first grey light of morning starts to creep across the hillside from the east, his concord with nature must end, turbulent dreams must be purged from his mind, and the day's realities must begin to bear down.

The lieutenant's bell tent is perched on the lower slopes of Kavkazia Hill, (in military parlance, Hill 107), and overlooks the airfield near Maleme village in north-west Crete. He reflects that his camp-bed – which is set in a slit trench some twelve inches deep – has afforded a less than luxurious night. Sleep in his one-man tent has been fitful as troubled dreams have struggled with jumbled memories. The night has seemed long and cold, and his consequent fatigue will not be eased by the imperative clang of a requisitioned church bell that, before long, will demand stand to. However, this should not occur for some minutes yet.

In the residue of starlight he tries to focus his eyes on the khaki sides of his tent, but the predominant gloom means he has to feel for his service-issue .45 Webley revolver placed carefully beneath his makeshift pillow. He checks the revolver, then concludes that his best course will be to remain still in the tent. He will await the church bell's summons. This should come at around 0515 hours; before that time, unnecessary movements outside the tent might incur the wrath of night sentries. He will have, therefore, a few moments of scarce quiet to meditate the problems ahead and to contemplate the curious circumstances of his present situation. Recent events have seen him assume a role more akin to infantry officer than career naval officer.

He remembers back to the period, some four or so months ago, when his cabin on HMS *Illustrious* had offered a rather more agreeable form of accommodation. On board ship, his life was regulated by familiar naval routines, and his duties revolved around those of a Fleet Air Arm observer, while social life centred around the wardroom. Within the confines of his cabin he could display family photographs, his personal kit was tended by his marine servant, and his ship – the pride of the fleet – appeared unassailable, efficient, and, most importantly, secure.

The carrier's undoubted reputation for operational effectiveness had imbued a sense of confidence in her crew; the men had felt able to cope with just about anything the enemy might throw at them. However, they were not prepared for the scale or the ferocity of the Stuka attacks on 10th January 1941. The ship came close to destruction on that day, and with sadness the lieutenant reflects on the numbers of colleagues lost. He ponders his own narrow escape, and remembers how the ship's fearsome battles had resulted in her departure from the Mediterranean theatre for reconstruction in the USA. The disbursement of her crew led in his own case to an appointment as naval liaison officer to the Royal Air Force in the Western Desert.

Posted to the staff of an air commodore, Lieutenant Sutton's duties included the drafting of orders for naval squadrons involved in desert operations. Placed in a situation of overview for the first major advance of General Wavell's troops against Italian forces, the lieutenant remembers this as a fascinating period. He recalls how the air commodore (a flying ace from World War One) had liked to keep his army and naval liaison officers close at hand for meetings, as a result of which these officers gained particular insight into the conduct of desert air operations. When, eventually, air superiority over the Italians was established, General Wavell's troops were facilitated in their advance through Libya towards Benghazi.

Allied headquarters was set up at Benghazi where a hotel on the sea front was designated as living quarters for officers. As a junior officer, he was confined to the back of the building in a small room normally reserved for chambermaids. Senior officers meanwhile occupied the best rooms with fine views across the sea front. However, he remembers the bedraggled-looking collection of wing commanders and group captains at breakfast one morning after a night of heavy air raids. The senior officers' grand sea-front rooms had taken the full force of enemy bombs while his own humble room at the back of the building had remained virtually unscathed.

When at Benghazi, he received information from desert wanderers – Arabs, Bedouins and the like – that Germans were in the area. He discussed this with officers at the naval headquarters in Alexandria, but the staff officer to the flag officer told him: "Sutton, you're getting windy. For God's sake pull yourself together, man. There are no Germans in North Africa."

"I've received information, sir…"

"There are no Germans in North Africa and that is that. Now get on and do your job properly."

A day or so passed after which a signal from naval headquarters in Alexandria was sent to Benghazi: 'Lieutenant Sutton to report to the commander-in-chief forthwith.'

As a communications aircraft was about to leave for Alexandria, the lieutenant was taken on board. Unfortunately, however, there was insufficient time for him to smarten up, even though he was conscious of Admiral Cunningham's reputation as a punctilious man and a martinet. The lieutenant therefore remained in his desert gear for the flight and for his subsequent arrival at the naval headquarters. Taken directly to the commander-in-chief's suite of offices, the lieutenant's overall appearance, his unsavoury clothing – unwashed for weeks – incurred Admiral Cunningham's instant wrath: "How *dare* you come to see your commander-in-chief when you are dressed like that?"

"I'm very sorry, sir, but I received a signal that I was to report to you forthwith."

"And 'forthwith' means that you appear in front of me dressed like that?"

Just now, in the gloomy, pre-dawn light of his tent, the lieutenant grimaces as he recalls the admiral's ruddy face, the stern line of mouth, and watery blue eyes that gave no quarter while the lieutenant received what he would describe later as 'the biggest blasting of my life'.

However, although the admiral was known for his explosive temper, he was known, too, for other, less forbidding characteristics. These included an unexpected kindness, an engaging, almost boyish, sense of humour. When he eventually calmed down and when the source of the problem (poor inter-service communication) had been identified, Admiral Cunningham was keen to move on to one of his favourite topics of conversation: life on board naval destroyers. The lieutenant recalls that by the time he was dismissed, he and the admiral had seemed on good terms.

Shortly after his return to Benghazi (and unconnected with the commander-in-chief incident) the lieutenant was told that he was to be posted away from the Western Desert to join the staff of the Royal Air Force commander in Greece, Air Vice-Marshal J H D'Albiac. He recollects the ominous briefings on the situation in Greece. A speedy and ruthless campaign in the Balkans was predicted, judging by grim images of last month's onslaught by Nazi forces. Within two days of the start of the Nazi invasion, the Yugoslav army had ceased to exist as a coherent force. In Greece, disaster struck on the first night when Luftwaffe bombers hit an ammunition ship in Piraeus harbour. The resultant blast, which flattened the dock installation and devastated the town, was recorded by an American aid worker and his wife in Athens:

'The whole sky flamed over Piraeus, an unearthly brilliance silhouetted the calm Parthenon in a stark, ghostly beauty. The continuing explosion left my wife and myself with our wits shaken, speechless and with a sense of the world's end. From neighbouring houses came sounds of maids screaming and the wild cries of a macaw. Nothing in the sound effects of catastrophe in Hollywood movies could match the crashing thunder, the crackling individual blasts under the greater roar, the howl of dogs and human shrieks… the blast broke plate glass windows eleven miles away. It is a great piece of luck for Hitler for it has given a terrific impression of German power and the awfulness of German-waged war.'

The lieutenant recalls how the atmosphere in Greece had swung rapidly from elation at the country's successes against the Italians to stunned disbelief at the swift havoc wrought by the Germans. A new attitude of defeatism began to afflict the Greek government. Under General Metaxas, the right-wing dictator known for his pro-German sympathies in the First World War, Greece had maintained a precarious neutrality.

The country, however, was strategically and financially bound to Britain, and the Greek royal family had close British connections. Last month, matters rose to a climax when the chief of staff, General Papagos, asked the British to withdraw in order to spare his country further suffering. Just two days later, Metaxas's successor, Prime Minister Koryzis, returned home from a meeting with his Cabinet. Evidently appalled by the deteriorating military situation, the prime minister retired to his bedroom and locked the door. A shot was heard. Staff rushed up to break into the room where they found Koryzis with a small icon of Our Lady of

Tenos in one hand, his gun in the other.

There were further ominous goings-on, such as sinister rumours, for example, that pictures of Hitler and Goebbels had appeared on the desk of the Athens police chief, and the country was in the process of betrayal by Nazi fifth columnists, and reports that General Tsolakoglou had surrendered the Army of the Epirus to the Germans.

With such a background no wonder the Royal Air Force and the Fleet Air Arm in the region had come under such exceptional pressures. There were other grave implications. Despite a rush to strengthen the air units in Greece, this had been at the expense of the build-up of squadrons elsewhere. Early in the New Year, the chief of the air staff, Air Chief Marshal Sir Charles Portal, had declared that:

'the foundation on which we should base our assistance to Greece is Crete, which must be held at all costs. Strong air forces established there would both delay the German advance...and be well sited for covering our air support to Turkey.'

However, even though the month before last, in March, the strength of the Royal Air Force in Greece had risen to the equivalent of some eighty serviceable aircraft with more in reserve, the RAF presence in Crete had been altogether inadequate. Fighter aircraft protection for the island had been left to a rag-bag collection of Fleet Air Arm aircraft at Maleme with Gladiators, Fulmars, and a few American Brewsters, renowned for engine problems.

Meanwhile the squadrons sent to the Greek mainland had been overwhelmed by the strength of Luftwaffe opposition. Nine days after the Nazis had entered Greece, a squadron of Blenheim aircraft (113 Squadron) had lost *all* of its aircraft to strafing Messerschmitts. On that same day, the lieutenant's new boss, Air Vice-Marshal D'Albiac, had informed his superiors that he had just forty-six serviceable aircraft left and that the shortage of defensible airfields meant that these machines risked destruction on the ground.

The scene was encapsulated by a young pilot (the writer Roald Dahl) when he arrived in Greece with a replacement Hurricane fighter from Egypt. Stiff and fatigued after a long flight, Dahl was harangued by a Royal Air Force corporal:

"I don't see the point of it...you bring a brand-new kite...straight from the factory and you bring it all the way from ruddy Egypt to this godforsaken place and what's goin' to 'appen to it? All the way across the Med to this soddin' country and for what?"

"What *is* going to happen to it?" asked Dahl, a bit taken aback by the corporal's outspoken outburst.

"I'll tell you what's goin' to 'appen to it," went on the corporal, working himself up. "Crash, bang, wallop! Shot down in flames! Explodin' in the air! Ground-strafed by the One-O-Nines right 'ere where we're standin' this moment! Why this kite won't stand one week in this place. None of 'em do! If you'd any sense at all, you'd have stayed right where you were back in old Egypt."

A mere eighteen Hurricanes had remained to cover the army's evacuation from mainland Greece last month. On the first morning of withdrawal, twelve fighters were sent up to fly over Athens in order to boost Greek morale. The machines became embroiled in air battles with over *200* Luftwaffe machines. Twelve versus 200! As one pilot recorded later: 'The sky was so full of aircraft that half my time was spent in actually trying to avoid collision.' In a battle of ludicrous odds, and incredible valour, five Hurricanes and four Allied pilots were lost, with twenty-two Messerschmitts destroyed. Three days later, the Luftwaffe caught remnants of the Royal Air Force at an airstrip near Argos:

'In utter impotence our pilots watched thirty to forty Me 110s silence the Bofors guns then pour bullets into the dispersed aircraft before turning their attention to the airmen and troops in the olive groves. It was a leisurely performance that occupied some forty minutes. At the end of it, thirteen Hurricanes had been destroyed on the ground and one in the air.'

The evacuation of the Royal Air Force had followed at dawn the next morning. Just seven surviving fighter aircraft took off from the Greek mainland and any remaining pilots were crammed into a small communications aircraft. These men escaped to Crete with virtually nothing apart from the clothes on their backs. One of their number would comment later: 'The whole thing was a cock-up...we should never have gone into Greece at all.'

The campaign had cost the Royal Air Force vital resources. Over 200 aircraft were lost, and of the personnel killed, captured or taken prisoner, 150 were aircrew. Anger about the RAF's performance in Greece was widespread and summed up in a piece of popular doggerel penned by an unknown Australian:

We marched and groaned beneath our load,
Whilst Jerry bombed us off the road.
He chased us here, he chased us there,
The bastards chased us everywhere.

And whilst he dropped his load of death
We cursed the bloody RAF.
And when we heard the wireless news,
When portly Winston aired his views –
The RAF was now in Greece
Fighting hard to win the peace;
We scratched our heads and said: 'Pig's arse,'
For this to us was just a farce,
For if in Greece the air force be –
Then where the bloody hell are we?

As often soldiers would link the Fleet Air Arm and the Royal Air Force as if distinction did not exist. Even in naval circles there had been a poor understanding of the Fleet Air Arm's activity in the Greek campaign. This, in part, had been caused by the clandestine nature of operations from an airfield in Albania. The airfield, in what was known as the 'Valley of Paramythia', was in enemy-held territory and Air Vice-Marshal D'Albiac had briefed 815 Squadron personnel of the crucial need for secrecy. "It would be better," said the air vice-marshal, "to lose an entire Swordfish squadron than to give away the position of the RAF's secret airfield."

No wonder, then, the Swordfish crews were wary as they flew around Paramythia. A pilot who realised that he was being shadowed one day, wrote later:

'I was at about 5,000 feet over Corfu when my observer shouted: "Fighters astern – on both sides!" A hasty glance over my shoulder revealed two Italian CR 42s. I saw them clearly in the glare of the sun, two little black squares tearing down towards my stern. I jettisoned my torpedo immediately (I learned later that it blew a sizeable hole in the south-west corner of Corfu) and as the Fiats opened fire I stood the Swordfish on its tail. The enemy bullets missed ahead and the Fiats spun over onto their backs and nearly collided.

'In double-quick time I dived to sea level...I have never dived a Swordfish so close to the vertical before, nor pulled out so close to the sea. In the dive, I kept the throttle almost fully open and the engine screamed in protest...I only just missed the sea and I had to do a steep climbing turn to avoid it. This blacked-out the observer for a few seconds.

'The Fiats then made a fatal error: they had recovered from their inverted spins and had climbed to attack again but they came in together, side by side. I dived to water level again...built up speed... then climbed vertically with the throttle closed. I let my aircraft go slightly over the vertical in a tightly stalled upward half of a loop then jammed the throttle wide open and rolled sideways into a stalled turn. At the commencement of that turn I was just in time to see two big splashes as both Italians spun into the sea.'

Lieutenant Sutton sighs. In the ongoing shrill of birdsong he still listens out for sounds of ominous accompaniment. At present, though, as all seems normal his mind flickers back again to the recent events in Greece. He realises that these had involved mainly hazard and disaster, although he recalls one incident with amusement. In the middle of last month, towards sunset and after a supper of corned beef and gin, aircrew were admiring the mountainous scenery as they sat peacefully on the grass outside their mess at Paramythia's secret airfield. Suddenly, however, when a cry was picked up – 'Aircraft approaching!' – eyes had turned to observe a twin-engined machine with wheels and flaps lowered.

"It's a Jerry Junkers 88!"

At this, all had scrambled to their feet before racing, revolvers in hand, to arrest the interloper. Fortunately, as matters turned out, there were no Bofors guns or other forms of heavy airfield defence. After the Ju 88's landing run, the new commanding officer of 815 Squadron (Torrens-Spence) had wrenched open the machine's door, thrust his revolver inside the cabin, and yelled that everyone should put their hands up. However, when he checked the cabin, Torrens-Spence found just three passengers, all of them smartly dressed. One of them stood up to introduce himself: "I am King Peter of Yugoslavia and that gentleman," he pointed, "is my prime minister."

"And I am Father Christmas," said Torrens-Spence. "Now come on, get out, with your hands up."

As the three men stepped into the evening sunlight, onlookers immediately recognised the king's face. A somewhat chastened Torrens-Spence then invited the king and his retinue to visit the officers' mess where royal amounts of gin were on offer. Regretfully, the prime minister had succumbed to the gin and by the time the Ju 88 was refuelled and ready for departure to Athens, he had to be carried back to his aircraft. The episode had caused great amusement within Fleet Air Arm circles but there was a serious side: as the rogue Ju 88 manoeuvred up and down the 'Valley of Paramythia', the machine was spotted by the Luftwaffe. Shortly after the king's departure, a squadron of Heinkels flew around the valley and the airfield had to be…

Clang! – Clang! – Clang! The lieutenant reaches under his makeshift pillow, extracts his .45 Webley revolver, leans forward to pull aside the tent's entrance flap. In the gloomy half-light he spots shadowy figures hasten through the olive grove as men react to the cries of "Stand to!" that now accompany the echoing sounds of a church bell.

19

Stand To

As he clambers from his bell tent, Lieutenant Sutton struggles to adjust his eyes in the early light. In addition to his .45 Webley revolver, he carries an ex-World War One .300 Ross rifle, one of a shipment that arrived a few days ago. Soon, he joins others who scramble through undergrowth towards stand-to positions on the hillside as the defensive plans for Hill 107 are executed.

A period of tension now follows. All are aware of the imminence of Nazi invasion, that this will be heralded, in all probability, by an early-morning Luftwaffe attack. Men know that, despite the brave faces put on by Allied leaders, the plans for the defence of Crete have suffered from lack of foresight and the last-minute preparations have been rushed. The obvious signs of inadequate resources, the dearth of Allied fighter aircraft, of troops and equipment, have all emphasised a general sense of vulnerability. Despite the edict that Crete must be saved 'at all costs', men understand that a monumental struggle lies ahead if the Nazis are to be repelled.

Perhaps as individuals dwell on this and as the early-morning chill helps to clear drowsy heads, the memories of their evacuation from Greece, the consequent sense of defeat and disarray, will harden the purpose of those now involved in Crete's defence. Men's determination – their fighting spirits – will be roused as, in these pre-dawn moments, they allow individual experiences to spur resolve.

As he reflects on some of his own recent experiences in Greece, the lieutenant recalls an improbable incident that followed last month's visit of King Peter of Yugoslavia to Paramythia. When a number of Dornier seaplanes put down in a bay to the west of Athens, the machines had attracted extravagant volumes of anti-aircraft fire. In spite of this, little damage was done, fortunately as matters turned out, because the machines were, in fact, Yugoslav Dorniers, not German.

When the Yugoslav markings were recognised, and the flags were waved from cockpit windows, the firing ceased and the crews were rescued. A common tongue of broken French was established at which Lieutenant Sutton was co-opted to speak with the officer in charge, a Yugoslav lieutenant-colonel.

It was agreed that the flight of a dozen or so seaplanes should proceed the next day down to Suda Bay in Crete, for which the lieutenant would act as navigator. Early the next morning, therefore, as he sat in the lieutenant-colonel's aircraft ready to lead the others due south, the lieutenant took advantage of a pause in proceedings to recap the arrangements for the flight's safe conduct. These arrangements, however, soon proved flawed. As the Dorniers rose above the early morning mists a nearby convoy of ships opened fire without hesitation. The lieutenant's bad but urgent French ordered his pilot to land at once and to sit on the sea while the convoy passed. When the ships were out of sight, a second take-off was achieved and this time the seaplanes continued safely down to Crete. At the entrance to the Suda Bay harbour, where an old fort requisitioned by the Royal Navy was used as an identification point, the lieutenant told his pilot to circle while the other aircraft held line astern formation.

Regretfully, however, the troops who guarded Suda Bay – 'a windy and very trigger-happy lot' – found the presence of Dornier aircraft an irresistible target. As it was still early, the duty naval staff were slow to react, and the lieutenant recalls how his attempts to lighten the proceedings with comments along the lines of "silly old fort" were unappreciated by the Yugoslav pilots who struggled to dodge 'friendly' bullets. When the naval staff had finally turned up, the lieutenant fired the agreed recognition signal of the day. He was given authority to proceed, although the seaplanes' onward flight to mooring buoys proved to be 'highly eventful'. Fortunately, just one seaplane got into difficulties and this machine had to be beached while the others secured themselves to mooring buoys. The crews were then collected by launch before being taken to a flying boat tender ship.

Meanwhile, the lieutenant was left with the problem of his return flight to Athens. After telephone calls to a number of officers, he spoke eventually with the pilot of an aircraft bound for Athens. The pilot agreed to accept him as a passenger on condition that the lieutenant would man the aircraft's rear gun. "Delighted," said the lieutenant who suddenly realised that, apart from the pilot himself, he would be alone on board. Nevertheless, the flight to Athens was without incident, although after landing the two were surprised to be greeted with energetic gesticulations from Royal Air Force ground crews. The two aircrew waved back politely. At this, the ground crews' gestures became frantic. Within seconds, swarms of Luftwaffe Me 109 aircraft swooped down to attack the airfield. As the lieutenant and his pilot dived for cover, they reached safety just before their aircraft was hit and consumed by fire.

The affair, reflects the lieutenant, was a harsh reminder of the perils faced by the Royal Air Force and Fleet Air Arm aircrews in Greece. As he ponders this, he thinks about the unjust way in which troops openly articulate their disgust at the airmen's efforts. Allied pilots and crewmen have demonstrated almost suicidal bravery in the face of preposterous odds, but the troops still express bitterness. With the rout of Allied forces from mainland Greece and with German attention now focused on Crete, the Luftwaffe has wreaked havoc in recent days. By yesterday, just five Allied fighter aircraft were left to defend the entire island of Crete: two Hurricanes and two Gladiators at Heraklion; and a single Hurricane here at Maleme.

In the officers' mess, the lieutenant has listened to discussions on the remarkable incident of a few days ago when low-flying Me 109s had struck Maleme airfield. The new commanding officer of the Royal Air Force's 33 Squadron, Squadron Leader Edward Howell, had been in conversation with one of his non-commissioned officers at the time of the attack. The squadron leader, although an experienced flying instructor, had not flown Hurricanes before and was being briefed, therefore, on the operation of flight and other controls.

When he noticed the two pilots in adjacent aircraft take off in a hurry, he waved away his sergeant and prepared to start the Hurricane's engine. As the engine kicked into life, the attendant aircraft fitter quickly pulled away the external starter battery connector, then dashed off. In his own words, the squadron leader later described how he thought: 'This is efficiency, the boys run about their business! Then I looked up. Through the subsiding dust, I saw the others twisting and turning among a cloud of Messerschmitt 109s.'

Subsequent events were related by a squadron airman:

'There were so many Messerschmitts it was impossible to keep track of them. Everything was yellow tracer and crackling cannon…109s swept past the CO on either side of him before he was airborne. Others came in on his starboard quarter just as he came "unstuck". Two Germans flashing past his nose left him in their slipstream. The Hurricane dropped violently in the bumpy air, then, miraculously unscathed, carried on. It kept low and headed for the protection of the hills.'

In normal circumstances, muses Lieutenant Sutton, a pilot's first flight on type should allow him to become familiar with the aircraft, the machine's quirks, good points and bad, and provide an opportunity to observe the local area. On that day, however, matters were far from normal. Nonetheless, despite the circumstances of his baptism by fire, the intrepid squadron leader had managed to shoot down a Messerschmitt of Luftwaffe unit 4/JG77. Sadly, his colleagues had fared less well: one pilot was shot down into the sea, although he survived; the other, Sergeant Ripsher, had died when hit by a burst of 'friendly' anti-aircraft fire as he attempted to crash-land his crippled Hurricane.

The lieutenant suddenly picks up the sound of distinctive New Zealand accents in the distance. A military voice barks instructions; men in their stand-to positions shout acknowledgement. A pause ensues, followed by more yells. The return of normality is signified by the resumption of birdsong, now accompanied by clatters from the airfield. An aircraft, it seems, is being manoeuvred in preparation for flight. As men listen from their stand-to positions, the prevalent air of apprehension begins to rise.

Lieutenant Sutton tightens the grip on his rifle as, within his mind, he goes over details of the local defensive plan. In his job as airfield adjutant, he has become reasonably well acquainted with the chief author of this plan, Colonel Andrew, who commands the 22nd New Zealand Battalion. Colonel Andrew has responsibility for the immediate task of airfield defence, and the lieutenant has found the colonel's directness a characteristic that might be expected of a professional soldier and holder of the Victoria Cross.

Noted for his hard-bitten approach and for his determined attitude, Colonel Andrew has risen through the ranks. From time to time, the colonel and the lieutenant have been flown together in a Swordfish aircraft in order to examine airfield defences from the air. During these flights, the colonel has revealed a strict eye for detail: he has emphasised that in the preparation of defensive measures, soil should be dispersed so as to leave no sign of disturbance, slit trenches should be camouflaged so the edges could not be seen, tracks should be suitably covered, and vehicles disguised. Lieutenant Sutton has admired the colonel's meticulous approach which has ensured that his battalion's defensive positions are difficult to spot from the air.

Even at ground level, as the lieutenant now tries to identify specific positions, these are hard to make out. He stares through the natural camouflage provided by olive trees but the defences remain well concealed, especially in the feeble light of dawn. Despite the lack of visible evidence, the lieutenant is aware that three companies – A, B and D – have been deployed on the slopes of Hill 107 from where men command two points of strategic significance: the airfield runway; and the iron bridge that carries the coastal road across the dry bed of the Tavronitis river. C Company has been positioned around the airfield perimeter with headquarters to the rear of the village of Pyrgos.

Colonel Andrew's battalion is supported by a few artillery weapons and by two heavy tanks dug in on the forward slopes of the hill. In addition, a number of men from miscellaneous units – the Fleet Air Arm, the Royal Air Force, and a detachment of Royal Marines from the Mobile Naval Base Defence Organisation – provide extra personnel in a situation where the shortage of manpower and equipment is every bit as chronic as for the ill-fated Greek campaign.

There is little wonder, thinks the lieutenant, that the colonel's plan is undermined by the lack of available back up. The nearest support units are some two miles away, to the south-east, where Colonel Leckie's 23rd New Zealand Battalion is dug in around the village of Dhaskaliana in the foothills above the coastal road.

Higher up is the 21st New Zealand Battalion, around Kondomari, under Lieutenant-Colonel Allen but this battalion suffered badly during the Greek campaign and is currently at half strength. Behind these units, a detachment of New Zealand engineers armed as infantry and a New Zealand Field Punishment Centre guard the coastal zone near Modi. Further east, around Platanias, is the 28th (Maori) Battalion under Colonel Dittmer.

Lieutenant Sutton has been briefed on the contingency plans if support is required in an emergency. Colonel Andrew has instructions to contact Colonel Leckie by telephone but if that fails, flares should be fired in a prearranged sequence: white-green-white. Colonel Leckie's orders are to hold his position although he has to be ready to counter-attack if needed. These counter-attacks could take place either towards the beach, or towards Maleme airfield, or towards the area held by the engineers.

Lieutenant-Colonel Allen's tasks seem equally ambitious, and just as ambiguous: he has to hold his position, but he must be ready to move to support the 22nd New Zealand Battalion in the event of an attack on Hill 107 from beyond the River Tavronitis. Alternatively, Lieutenant-Colonel Allen may have to move his men sideways to take up positions vacated by Colonel Leckie's 23rd Battalion if the latter receive orders to counter-attack. All of these units fall under the command of Brigadier James Hargest, the officer in charge of the 5th New Zealand Brigade which controls the western half of the Maleme sector. A farmer in civilian life and a member of the New Zealand parliament, the fifty-one-year-old brigadier is a veteran of the Gallipoli campaign of 1915-1916. This evening, when he will contemplate the sunset over Cape Spatha, the brigadier will be joined by a fellow New Zealand officer who later will recall:

'Brigadier Hargest stared northward across the sea from which any airborne attack would come. Then he said quietly: "I don't know what lies ahead. I only know that it produces in me a sensation I never knew in the last war. It is not fear. It is something quite different, something which I can only describe as dread." I knew exactly what he meant. His was the reaction of a man of proven bravery to the mystique, indeed the mystery which seemed to surround Germany's staggering success in the field.

'We were in the path of a military machine which had smashed Poland in a matter of days, had overwhelmed France, Belgium, Holland in a matter of weeks, and had swept through Yugoslavia and Greece like an avalanche. In the Western Desert only a few German tanks and a previously little-known general, Erwin Rommel, had been needed to rout the British Army. Now, over this golden blue horizon, these same apparently irresistible forces were massing to descend on us.'

Just now, as he gazes through the dark of the olive grove, Lieutenant Sutton feels a sense of gloom as he reflects on the precarious nature of local defensive measures. Brigadier Hargest's and senior officers' urgent requests for artillery, tanks and other reinforcements to be sent across from Egypt have received meagre response: some 100 artillery guns have reached the island, although only eighty-five of these have proved serviceable.

Furthermore, as many of the guns have been captured from the Italians and lack sights, Allied crews have to construct makeshift aiming devices of wood and chewing gum, or else will have to peer down barrels in order to take aim. Of the tanks requested, six heavy infantry tanks and sixteen light tanks have been detached to Crete from Egypt but evidently most of these have been described as 'desert-battered hulks hastily patched up in Waadian workshops'.

These and other factors, notably a shortage of equipment, even basic accoutrements such as entrenching tools, have created serious difficulties. As with others across the hillside, he has had to prepare his own defensive position by scooping away soil with his steel helmet, a time-consuming process in the rocky ground. Most of the troops now marshalled to face the Germans are men who, in the haste of the mainland Greece evacuation, had been forced to leave behind equipment. As one Australian would explain later:

'I had a blanket and a greatcoat but for a week or more I shared the blanket with three others. I slipped into the town of Chania and bought a brush and a razor. Except for a table knife, that was all my equipment. Half a battalion arrived with no boots at all. Their ship had been torpedoed; a cruiser came alongside and they were told to get on board: "Take your boots off, leave your rifle behind and jump." So they did and they arrived in Crete with not even the most basic equipment.'

Along with these troops, reflects the lieutenant, the numbers of diverse individuals (Greek evacuees, Cypriot pioneers, administrators, clerks from field postal companies, men who have lost their units, and deserters) have caused additional problems. Some of these men have lived like bandits in the hills and olive groves and violent behaviour has damaged relations with local Cretans. There have been reports of a British officer who attempted to intervene when he spotted a drunken Australian trying to rob a stall in Chania, Crete's capital. When the Australian produced a looted German pistol, the officer was compelled to draw back. Even Prince Peter of Greece (who has ended up in Crete after his flight via the 'Valley of Paramythia') was threatened by an armed gang in a wine shop and had to be rescued by military police. A curfew was introduced and field courts martial established, but the situation has been slow to improve.

This sorry scenario, combined with the escalation of Luftwaffe air attacks, had begun to shatter the resolve of one of the lieutenant's fellow officers. The officer, assigned as assistant to the senior naval officer at Maleme (Commander Beale), eventually took to the relative safety of the hills, refusing to return except for occasional visits to the officers' mess for food.

The commander had contemplated a trial by court martial for this officer, but decided instead to write an adverse report and to post him away. As a consequence, Lieutenant Sutton's job had changed from operations officer to airfield adjutant. He had been required to assume a variety of different tasks, most of which involved organisation of ground and air defences in the vicinity of Maleme's airfield.

It was shortly before the commencement of these new duties, reflects the lieutenant, that he became embroiled in an unfortunate incident. One day, he was in conversation with aircrew colleagues at their squadron dispersal site when a Cretan workman was spotted beneath the wing of a Fulmar fighter aircraft. The fellow, it seemed, had decided to shelter from the midday sun. However, as the loyalty of the local population was considered uncertain in the island's general atmosphere of unrest, Cretan workmen were banned from the airfield except for supervised construction work.

When the man was spotted, two armed guards were despatched to investigate. As the guards ran across, the workman was seen to drop something behind him. Wire clippers were found and an examination by engineers revealed deliberate acts of damage to the Fulmar's wing hinges, also to electrical and hydraulic connections. The Cretan workman was therefore arrested and handed over to nearby Australian infantry troops. The Australians were advised to take the suspected saboteur for interrogation by the Greek military authorities at headquarters in Chania. The Australians marched their prisoner off, but returned very soon. A discussion ensued:

"That was quick. What have you done with him? Has he escaped?"

"On, no. He's all right."

"What do you mean, 'all right'? What have you done with him?"

"For God's sake! You wanted him dealt with didn't you?"

"Well, yes."

"So we dealt with him, didn't we."

"How?"

"We took him to the village just down the road."

"And then?"

"We shot him, of course. Be assured, gentlemen: you won't have any more trouble from that village."

The incident had highlighted the unease felt by Allied troops, including the lieutenant himself, towards local Greeks and Cretans. (In time, though, this will change; and Sutton will describe them as 'magnificent friends'.) He recollects how the need for caution was illustrated by another unpleasant incident which occurred one evening, just before the pre-dusk stand to.

As he set about the inspection of night blackout and other defensive measures, he spotted a figure silhouetted against the light of an open window. At once, the lieutenant drew his .45 Webley pistol, crept up behind a man, and ordered: "Hands up!" to the individual seen to be staring into the operations hut. The lieutenant then marched the man to a detachment of New Zealanders and instructed them to contact the Greek military authorities in Chania. Later, he would learn that the suspected enemy agent, having refused to answer questions under interrogation, had been shot as a spy.

Suddenly, a particular racket from the airfield starts to echo across Hill 107. The lieutenant tries to peer through the olive grove towards the source of the commotion, but the pre-dawn light remains weak. Some distance away, a broad New Zealand voice yells a series of commands. Clangs and clicks of machinery ensue. All listen to an aircraft engine being fired up. The noise is followed by the rise of the engine note as the machine is manoeuvred, then the familiar sound of a Hurricane at full power for the take-off run. The roar of take-off fades as the machine disappears on a south-easterly course. An interlude of hush gradually intensifies the anxious atmosphere around Hill 107. Soon, however, the quiet spell is interrupted when men begin to distinguish another sound. All now brace themselves for action. Lieutenant Sutton re-tightens his grip on his .300 Ross rifle and he continues to stare through the olive grove as, emerging like some ogre from the deep, he picks up the escalating din of Messerschmitt 109s in the background.

20

Call of Duty

When Messerschmitt 109s commence their dawn strafing runs on the portentous day of Monday, 19th May 1941, the area around Maleme airfield erupts into an inferno of aircraft machine-gun fire and anti-aircraft fire. The assault lasts for some thirty or so minutes before Luftwaffe raiders disappear due north towards mainland Greece. At that point the all-clear is sounded and Allied personnel emerge from hideouts on the hillside. An atmosphere of excitement is still evident when men meet up and form groups to make their way down the hill in order to wash and shave before breakfast.

Personnel head for mess tents that comprise part of the Royal Air Force camp established on the lower slopes of Hill 107. The mess tents and other camouflaged constructions form the administrative heart of the camp and as men join up, conversations include, no doubt, expressions of alarm at the Hurricane's narrow escape. The last remaining fighter aircraft's departure has provoked a new mood of vulnerability which Lieutenant Sutton senses as he listens to apprehensive speculations.

At breakfast in the barn that now serves as the officers' mess, he chats with a sub-lieutenant. An initial sense of reserve eases when the sub-lieutenant starts to talk about home, about his girlfriend and his last meeting with her. The couple had felt uncomfortably aware of their limited time together. As he reminisces, the sub-lieutenant describes a party the couple had attended on his last period of leave. The party, a ceilidh dance, had been held in a village hall. Two kilted bagpipe players had welcomed guests and the sub-lieutenant smiles as he recollects his own kilt and those of other male guests. He recalls the shrill screams and laughter that had begun to fill the hall when inhibitions were thrust aside as dancing began and as feet stamped across the floor, arms linked and released, heads were thrown back to allow exuberant throats to yell ululating whoops.

The time was close to four in the morning when the party had broken up and then, under the heavy moon of an autumnal night, the sub-lieutenant and his girlfriend had strolled arm in arm, gloomily aware of their impending separation. The cold night air had cast away the happy mood stimulated by the dancing. The couple's spirits had become depressed as they talked about grim realities, the uncertainties ahead, the risks and difficulties of planning in wartime. The young sub-lieutenant hesitates. He glances at his breakfast companion, then reaches inside a pocket to extract a photograph which, proudly, he places on the breakfast table. The treasured, if dog-eared, picture reveals a young woman's smiling face, her dark curls ruffled by the wind. She seems happy, radiantly so, in her attractive dress which, in all probability and in view of wartime constraints, she has had to make herself.

The men's light-hearted chat quietens as they scrutinise the cheery depiction of future dreams; in a finite moment the photograph has captured the girlfriend's look, her soft cheeks and her shy smile. The men's unspoken thoughts seem to coincide: images of loved ones will be held by others across the expanses of Hill 107 and elsewhere. The photographs will emphasise the ironies confronted by the fighting man, the slim division between light and dark, ecstasy and doom, the fate over which individuals will have little control.

Conversation resumes as, coyly, the sub-lieutenant returns the photograph to his pocket. He asks the lieutenant about his wife, about other aspects of his home life, but time presses and before long, at the conclusion of their breakfast, both men stand up to leave. "Good luck," the lieutenant says as the two prepare for their separate duties.

"We'll need plenty of that."

"Of what?"

"Luck!"

"What's lined up for you, then?"

"I'm off to Prison Valley," the sub-lieutenant gestures towards the direction of the Aiya Valley where a small, white-washed jail is the dominant feature. "Commander Beale has a task for me there. How about you?"

"Same as yesterday, I suppose…supervision and improvement of airfield defences."

"Hasn't there been a bit of bother to do with the siting of Bofors guns? There was talk of it last night."

The lieutenant frowns. "Unfortunately, yes. In spite of Colonel Andrew's emphasis on the need for camouflage and concealment, the Bofors guns remain out in the open. The Bofors provide a cone of fire directly over the runway but this, of course, gives rise to the dilemma of guns and gunners exposed to Luftwaffe attacks. But there's another complication, too."

"Oh?"

"You may recall the event of a few days ago? One of our pilots – Sergeant Ripsher – attempted an emergency landing, but he was shot down by the Bofors."

"I remember – a tragic accident."

"As a result of it, the marine gunners have orders not to open fire without the prior permission of an officer. In view of the shortage of officers, this is proving rather problematic."

"So what's going to happen?"

The lieutenant shrugs. "Colonel Andrew has no jurisdiction over the local marine commander, Major Kay, who answers to the Mobile Naval Base Defence Organisation at Suda Bay. The colonel, understandably, is frustrated by the system of divided command. He's trying to get the matter resolved but progress is slow."

"The army, don't you think, can be disposed towards slow progress?" The two men grin as they move away from the officers' mess barn. Soon, when each goes his separate way, Lieutenant Sutton takes up a brisk pace while he heads for the operations set-up. As he walks along, the breakfast conversation still fresh in his mind, he is struck by the way individuals have the need just now to talk about home and happier times; many, no doubt, feel inclined to contemplate their mortality in the present exceptional circumstances. Indeed, a few weeks ago when he was still in Greece, following his return to Athens after the Yugoslav seaplane incident, he had reported to the senior air staff officer, a harassed group captain, who had greeted him brusquely with the words: "You back? I thought we'd got rid of you. Didn't you fly down to Crete?"

"Yes, sir, but I've come back. I'm still a member of your staff."

"Oh yes. I suppose you are. Hang on a minute, then, while we try to sort something out." The lieutenant had waited while the group captain retreated out of earshot for a discussion with colleagues. On his return, the senior air staff officer had seemed cagey. "I want you to report to the flying boat base tonight, at 2300 hours," he had said. "A special mission has been planned for tonight but I can't tell you anything about it at present. Get your things together; pack what you can, leave the rest behind. You'll be briefed tonight by staff at the flying boat base."

He had arranged to meet friends in Athens before he reported for duty that night. There was an eerie atmosphere present in Athens as he and his friends had supper and talked together for the last time in mainland Greece. The deserted streets, littered with burnt and burning paper as people destroyed their records before the Germans moved in, had seemed to echo with the ubiquitous sense of dread.

After supper, when he had bade a poignant farewell to his friends, the lieutenant was driven directly to the flying boat base where a squadron leader welcomed him: "So you're one of them are you?"

"I am?"

"Didn't you know?"

"Evidently not."

"Members of the Greek royal family are being evacuated tonight. You and two flight lieutenants have been detailed to act as escorts."

Preparations had followed and the lieutenant remembers how, at around midnight and when the royal entourage were driven up to the flying boat base, the very important persons were led by King George the Second's brother Paul and his wife Frederika (they became King and Queen of Greece when the divorced King George the Second died two years after the war). Other members had included Princess Alexandra (who would marry King Peter of Yugoslavia), the king's brother's two young children, Princess Sofia (later Queen of Spain) and Prince Constantine (later King of Greece). King George the Second himself had been flown in a separate aircraft with the gold stocks of the Bank of Greece, but amongst the flying boat party were the king's mistress (this was not generally known at the time) Mrs Britten-Jones and the king's uncle (an admiral in the Greek navy with a moustache described as 'a foot long either side of his face').

A number of equerries, nannies and general hangers-on had been in attendance also. Before the flying boat's departure the lieutenant had been required to assist with the transfer of heavy leather suitcases which, he assumed, contained the crown jewels. When the suitcases had been loaded, the passengers were boarded and the machine was cleared for take-off. The lieutenant recollects how, for the flight south, the passengers had been segregated: one cabin for the royal party, a separate cabin for the escorting officers, and others. The flight itself had been uneventful but tension rose as the flying boat approached Suda Bay. However, this time – unlike for the Yugoslav seaplanes – anti-aircraft gunners had been firmly briefed; the flying boat had landed safely before the machine was secured to a mooring buoy in Suda Bay.

It was at that point that plans had begun to go awry. Arrangements had been made for the collection of the passengers by boat, but the vessel had failed to materialise. Lieutenant Sutton had become increasingly anxious as dawn advanced, a time of day when the Germans were liable to attack. Unhappily conscious that a flying boat had been bombed and destroyed in a dawn raid just the day before, the lieutenant had volunteered to use his skills as a semaphore sender to try to make contact with the crew of a nearby sunken cruiser. In the greyness of the pre-dawn light, he could just make out the vessel, a victim of action by Italian torpedo boats. From the flying boat's cockpit, he had pointed the semaphore lamp to flash out the signal: 'PSBVIP' (naval parlance for: 'please send boat – very important persons').

'MRUHNB' had come the reply (much regret unable – have no boats). The cruiser crew had agreed, nevertheless, to communicate the urgency of the situation to the Royal Air Force. Quite soon, therefore, a flying boat tender craft had turned up to ferry the very important passengers ashore. This had worked well except that, as the flying boat tender was of modest size, the passengers had to be ferried off in small numbers and in accordance with rank: royal members first, followed by others.

All had been landed on a small wooden jetty, then left to stand about. Lieutenant Sutton, a little concerned about the Greek royal family's rather 'unroyal' treatment and about their forlorn appearance, consequently had decided that, as he knew the local geography, he should lead the party away from the waterfront and up the hillside. They would make for a stone hut requisitioned by the Royal Navy for the use of their naval officer in charge.

When the party had approached the darkened hut, the lieutenant had asked everyone to wait outside while he entered to negotiate suitable arrangements. When he'd knocked on the door a gruff voice had invited him to enter. He had stepped inside to find the duty officer busily laying out charts on a tabletop as he prepared for that morning's operations.

"Well?" the duty officer had been curt.

"Good morning."

"Oh yes: good morning. Well?"

"I have the Greek royal family outside."

"What?"

"The Greek royal family – they're outside."

"*What?*"

"Outside the door...the Greek royal family."

"What the hell are you on about?"

"The Greek royal family."

"For God's sake, man, don't bother me at this hour in the morning. Can't you see I'm busy? This is no time for practical jokes."

"The Greek royal family are waiting outside the door."

"What next? Kindly bugger off and pester someone else."

"The Greek royal family are outside, what else can I say? If you don't believe me – go and see for yourself."

A pause had ensued; the two had glared at each other before, in a sudden gesture, the duty officer had slammed the tabletop and stormed outside.

Within moments Lieutenant Sutton had heard: "Good God!"

"But…" The duty officer had faltered. "But…" The duty officer had then dashed back inside, his face now a paler shade as he stared at Lieutenant Sutton who repeated:

"The Greek royal family are outside."

"What the hell are we supposed to do with that little lot?"

"Any ideas?"

"God knows. Why've you brought 'em here? Are you mad? Are they mad? Am I mad? Are they hungry? Perhaps we'd better give 'em breakfast."

"Good plan. A full naval breakfast?"

"Why not?"

"They *must* be hungry."

Soon, the naval charts had been swept from tabletops and the tables had been rearranged for a breakfast feast. Stewards at a nearby mess had been alerted and unlikely amounts of coffee, toast, tinned fare, marmalade, sausages, beans, fried bread, general hotchpotch had been piled onto the tabletop. Before long, a mix of people, equally unlikely, had sat down to tuck in to a 'thorough-going, gooey naval breakfast'. Breakfast, if less than sophisticated, had appeared to be enjoyed by one and all nonetheless. However, the enjoyment had been rudely disturbed halfway through the meal when the *brumph…brumph…brumph…*sound of anti-aircraft fire was picked up.

At once, several officers had hastened outside to see what was happening. By then the sun was low over the mountains and in the early light the officers could spot the silvery glint of aircraft wings as the machines banked. The officers, therefore, had hurried back to the hut where the duty officer had cried: "My lords, ladies and gentlemen…" he had paused, uncertain of the protocol "…I'm terribly sorry everyone, but we'll have to abandon breakfast immediately. Enemy aircraft are about to attack us. We'll have to take refuge in nearby trenches. Please follow me…"

Lieutenant Sutton, while he now thinks about the circumstances of that interrupted breakfast, remembers how he had spotted Princess Alexandra as she struggled with her young daughter, Princess Sofia. It had seemed that the two were being left behind in the general dash for safety. He therefore had grabbed Princess Sofia and tucked her under his arm as he ran towards the nearest trench into which he dived headfirst with Princess Alexandra in hot pursuit. All had crouched down inside the trench as bombs started to fall although it became clear quite quickly that the enemy's target was shipping in Suda Bay, not the royal party.

The bombers had taken their time; the lieutenant had taken the opportunity to look around him. Royalty had rubbed shoulders with local shepherds and in the trench, too, was the Greek admiral with his splendid uniform and his still-magnificent moustache, albeit by that stage somewhat battered.

The lieutenant had felt sympathy for the royal members' plight and he had admired their bravery, especially that of the young Princess Sofia. When the bombers had been seen to head north, the royal party and others had started to emerge from trenches. At that juncture, events had begun to happen fast. A cavalcade of large black Mercedes cars had been driven up, the Greek governor had stepped out of the lead car and scuttled across to greet the royal party. The royal members were ushered hastily into the cars but without any opportunity to thank or say farewell to their naval hosts. The lieutenant and his fellow officers had felt less than flattered by the Greek governor's attitude of annoyance at the royal family's treatment, as if the officers themselves had been to blame for the exposure of royal persons to the hazards of a danger zone.

The lieutenant suddenly checks his pace and glances up at the sky. He angles his head and listens for the racket of distant aircraft. Luftwaffe attacks have been heavy in recent days; today is unlikely to be different. He decides, however, that the sound is far off, and the immediate vicinity is not directly threatened. The Luftwaffe, of course, can be expected to attack Hill 107 at any time but just now their efforts appear to be concentrated against the Suda Bay area.

As he resumes his brisk walk towards the operations centre, the lieutenant reflects on the way his involvement with the royal exodus from mainland Greece had resulted in his own move to Crete. He had hoped for an onward transfer to Alexandria, but his naval superior officer, Commander Beale, had ordered him to remain in Crete where, for the time being at least, he would act as one of the operations officers co-ordinating the evacuation of squadrons from Greece. The commander had said he was sorry, he realised that the lieutenant had been chivvied about, but then so had everyone else. Thus it was that, in his new capacity, Lieutenant Sutton had been introduced to some of the senior army officers charged with Crete's defence, including Colonel Andrew, Brigadier Hargest, and the man in overall charge, General Bernard Cyril Freyberg.

The lieutenant recollects his sense of awe at meeting General Freyberg, a man decorated with the Victoria Cross and the Distinguished Service Order with two bars (further bars would follow). He was born into a large London family which had emigrated to New Zealand when he was just two years of age. Freyberg had seen action in the World War One Gallipoli campaign when he had been described as: 'a living legend when he swam ashore in the Dardanelles to light false beacons in a plan to deceive the Turks as to the landing beaches chosen by the Allied Expeditionary Force.'

The intrepid Freyberg, though, had yearned for the ultimate accolade: the award of the Victoria Cross. His aim had become a burning ambition, fulfilled in 1916 during the Battle of the Ancre when he was involved with the capture of the Beaucourt redoubt. Seriously wounded in the process, he had been evacuated to a dressing station where he had 'appeared with his head and eyes covered in blood-soaked bandages and all the colour gone from his face. Stretcher-bearers had taken him to the tent reserved for those not expected to survive and who were given no treatment other than painkilling drugs.'

By a twist of fate, however, Freyberg's life had been saved by the chance intervention of an unknown doctor. By the end of World War One, by which stage he had risen to the rank of temporary brigadier-general, Freyberg's war had concluded as it had begun, with an act of wanton boldness. Having led a cavalry raid against a key bridge, Freyberg had seized his objective intact, capturing three German officers and 100 men in the process. After the war, Freyberg had befriended Winston Churchill who had seemed fascinated by the general's feats. The two men had met at a country-house party in 1919 where Churchill had asked to see evidence of Freyberg's wounds. Unabashed, the general had stripped himself off to allow Churchill to count twenty-seven separate scars and gashes.

The hardened, even coarsened figure the lieutenant had expected to meet was, in fact, a man of keen intelligence with piercing, wide-set eyes that studied his naval assistant sharply. A large man, General Freyberg had exuded an air of confident boyishness, like an overgrown boy scout about to engage in some mischief. The general's voice had been unexpectedly high-pitched, his aura alert, with a strong hint of ready humour. The general's appointment as the commander of CREFORCE had caused controversy within army circles. Shortly after his arrival by cruiser at Suda Bay at the end of April, General Freyberg had met the commander-in-chief, General Wavell, who had revealed that Churchill himself wished Freyberg to take over as commander in Crete. The lieutenant remembers the positive tone of the new general's communiqué to his men: 'If he attacks us here in Crete, the enemy will be meeting our troops on even terms, and those of us who met his infantry in the last month ask for no better chance.'

Years later, Lieutenant Sutton will learn different truths. He will know that the above communiqué, designed to bolster the morale of troops, was one of three sent by General Freyberg at dusk on 1st May 1941.

One message would inform General Wavell that without the full support of the Royal Air Force and the Royal Navy, his men on Crete who lacked artillery, transport, even digging tools, could not hope to repel an invasion.

Another message, this time to the New Zealand government, would say:

'I feel it my duty to report the military situation in Crete. Decision has been taken in London that Crete must be held at all costs. Would strongly recommend you bring pressure to bear on highest plane in London to either supply us with sufficient means to defend the island or to review decision.'

If these messages had eased the sender's conscience, they had achieved little else. Other factors, unknown to most at the time, would add to the overall web of confusion that to this day still obscures the interpretation of events. Following a staff conference after his meeting with General Freyberg, General Wavell would ask his fellow general to accompany him on a private walk in the garden. During the walk, the commander-in-chief would tell General Freyberg that the Enigma decoding machine used by staff at Bletchley Park had intercepted German secret intelligence signals. Accordingly, the enemy's plans for the invasion of Crete were known. Future intercepts, code-named Ultra, would be supplied to Freyberg on a 'read and destroy' basis. After the war, Freyberg would claim that the emphasis was on the need for strict security, that:

'First, he was not to mention the existence of Ultra to anyone else on Crete. Secondly, he was never to take any action as a result of what he heard from Ultra alone. If the rule was not adhered to, there was a danger that the enemy might realise that his codes had been broken.'

Perhaps this may help to explain some of the baffling decisions made in Crete during the desperate days of May 1941. Nevertheless, if inputs from Ultra had tended to blur further the already shadowy world of intelligence and counter-intelligence, the situation was hardly helped by General Freyberg's misinterpretations. He remained tight-lipped about Ultra for the rest of his life; apart from death-bed revelations to his son, he took mysteries to the grave. Perhaps his keenness to conceal the secret of Ultra lay behind the muddled thinking and misunderstandings which were seminal to the collapse of the Allied campaign in Crete. General Fryeburg was said to be obstinate, at times wilfully obtuse, and it was: '...something of a joke amongst his fellow generals that if he grasped the wrong end of the stick he found it impossible to let go.' The official New Zealand history would record that: 'The conclusion is inevitable that General Freyberg began with a battle plan which gave his battalion commanders too much choice of role...and that in the battle itself he failed to give his commanders firm direction.'

Just now, as he continues his brisk pace towards the operations set-up, Lieutenant Sutton will be unaware of the impending breakdown of carefully-briefed contingency plans for counter-attack. Over the next few days, the commitment of General Freyberg and his brigadiers to their own plans will appear less than robust. This will lead to the battle's turning point, centred around errors of judgement made in the western Maleme sector commanded by Brigadier Hargest.

An unnecessary Allied retreat from the Maleme area will follow, one that will surprise no-one more than the Germans. After this, the balance will begin to weigh in Germany's favour. When combined with the appalling acts of dishonour and foul revenge shown by the invaders, the scene will be set for a tragedy bound to afflict the island for generations ahead.

With the benefit of hindsight, some have accused General Freyberg and his officers of World War One mentalities unsuitable for the fast-moving Crete campaign. These were brave men who faced daunting tasks. Maybe unreasonable, unrealistic demands placed on them were a step too far, one, indeed, well above and beyond the call of duty.

21

Long Legacies

As he approaches the operations hut in the Royal Air Force camp, Lieutenant Sutton views the arrangement with a critical eye. He remembers his efforts of a few weeks ago when, in the interests of security, he had pressed for the operations set-up to be sited in a prepared dugout on the side of Hill 107. Greek workmen were allotted to the task but progress had been slow in the rocky soil. Eventually the workmen were diverted away from the scheme when the preparation of runways was deemed of greater priority. With a sigh, the lieutenant recalls how, when his project was abandoned, the half-finished operations room was dubbed 'Alfie's Folly'.

The lieutenant reflects gloomily on the dilemmas of recent weeks. Since he became involved with the organisation of airfield defensive measures at Maleme, these have been designed within the overall guidelines of General Freyberg's defence plan. However, constant air attacks and the rushed nature of the plans have created considerable difficulties. Furthermore, the general's strategy, which divides Crete into four self-contained sectors (Heraklion, Rethymnon, Suda Bay and Maleme), has its weak points. This is especially the case for the latter sector, commanded by Brigadier Edward Puttick who reports directly to General Freyberg. Regretfully the point of greatest weakness is probably within his own area, the western half of the Maleme sector which is controlled by the 5th New Zealand Brigade under Brigadier Hargest.

A number of factors have exacerbated this situation. For example, the local Cretans, who by nature make good guerrilla fighters, have appeared keen to fight the Germans. The Allied hierarchy, however, has shown marked reluctance to organise a Cretan Home Guard or to arm headstrong locals. Another cause of aggravation is the islanders' feeling of bitterness towards King George the Second, especially due to the way he had escaped from mainland Greece while the Cretan Division was left behind.

Now, Greek troops from the mainland have been allocated to the Maleme area but their morale is low and many suffer from malaria. Most of these men have to make do with ancient Austrian rifles with just ten rounds each. Further dilemmas arise because of the shortage of transport and due to poor standards of accessible communications: few radios are available and the local telephone system is primitive and liable to be cut off at any time.

Such issues have influenced the organisation of airfield defence, an area where, as elsewhere, the general lack of preparation has impeded the Royal Air Force men who now run the airfield assisted by naval personnel. On the 17th of last month, when Wing Commander G R Beamish had assumed command of two flight lieutenants and seventeen other ranks in Chania, his appointment was timely. Before he took over, the Royal Air Force in Crete was under the command of a junior officer.

The wing commander's efforts have been stoical but his problems mounted as Greece was evacuated and as Luftwaffe attacks began to concentrate on Crete. Just recently, airfield personnel were briefed on the need to become more involved with airfield defence, yet these men remain under-equipped and under-trained as infantrymen. When Lieutenant Sutton made arrangements for individuals to be given basic infantry training, it soon became clear that some of the men had never before received instruction on how to handle a rifle. Now, though, with the disappearance of the island's last fighter aircraft, the role of infantryman will become the main task of these airfield personnel.

The lieutenant ponders how matters of poor preparation, and inadequate planning, have afflicted past campaigns as if such problems were an inherent part of Britain's entry into war. The annals are littered with examples of lack of foresight; historical bad habits persist and the lessons of history fail to be learned. Even at the so-called height of the British Empire, when the spark that flamed the Crimean campaign was struck in Bethlehem, lack of preparation had meant that Allied forces were handicapped from the earliest stages.

Such conditions, reflects the lieutenant, had fuelled the background to calamity, including one of the most famed of military disasters, the charge of the Light Brigade. Eighty-seven years ago, in October 1854, when bad planning, poor leadership and unfortunate luck had conspired to send the Light Brigade on its charge of catastrophe, then as now, recalls the lieutenant, sleeping rough in the same clothes for days and weeks on end, bitter winds and nights, sleep interrupted by alerts, had progressively eroded the troops' physical and mental stamina.

Lieutenant Sutton glances over his shoulder. As he gazes up at the sky, he becomes aware of a petty officer who dashes up: "Sir! We'd best head for that trench over there." At once, the men break into a run then hurl themselves into a nearby trench. They listen to the distinctive clang of Hill 107's air-raid warning bell become gradually drowned by the approaching shriek of Messerschmitts. As they crouch for protection, those in the trench form themselves into defensive curls, cover their heads with their hands, and wait.

22

Air Raid

With the Luftwaffe's advantage of local air superiority, their air raid is protracted and relentless. The German pilots carry out their missions in a leisurely routine while those below are forced to endure the consequences. Aircraft pens, Bofors anti-aircraft positions, other defensive sites are bombed and strafed but it appears that the pilots have been briefed to avoid damage to the runways which, before long, might be needed by the Germans themselves.

In his trench, Lieutenant Sutton tries to observe the proceedings from a position of relative safety. He avoids the temptation to stare directly at aircraft (the whites of faces can be spotted readily from the air) but at an opportune moment, as he looks around to identify others in the trench, he gives a nod of appreciation to the petty officer who had warned him of the Messerschmitts' approach. Does he recognise the man from days in Greece? He's not sure. Many of the faces in the trench, a mix of air force and naval personnel, seem familiar although most, at this moment, look mud splattered and not overly inclined to show friendly recognition.

The ground shudders; aircraft roar overhead; chaos prevails as the Luftwaffe bombers spill venom out of a quiet sky. RAT-A-TAT-A-TAT! BOOM! Machine guns rattle, bombs blast, men's nerves are shattered. BOOM! Each bomb looks nearer than the last. BOOM! BOOM! Every explosion appears to heighten an individual's trepidation and sense of growing isolation. BRRRRRRRRRRUMPH...BOOM! BANG! Are we the last on earth? SCREEEEEECH! BOOOM! Surroundings lie paralysed, signs of life eliminated along with honour, credence, and faith.

Yet men survive. Lieutenant Sutton wonders about personal ruses to maintain sanity, to stay stoical, disciplined, not to succumb. Perhaps, like the sub-lieutenant at breakfast time, an individual will think about the woman whose picture he holds within his breast pocket.

BOOM! BANG! BRRRRUMPH! That one was close. What next? BOOM! That is what's next. CRRRUNCH...CRASH!...violence, hatred, death.

BANG...CRRRRASH! The bombs remind men of ordeals in Greece. Why were such ordeals allowed to develop? Ask Churchill, ask Roosevelt. Ask Hitler, ask Mussolini. Mussolini: the arch-opportunist who took his chance all right when he decided to invade Greece last autumn. He consulted Hitler, so it was said, but the foolish *Führer* raised no objections as long as the action was 'quick and decisive'. When the Greek leader Metaxas was awakened early one autumn morning last year, he was presented with an ultimatum that required an undeniably quick and decisive reply. The Italian ambassador harangued Metaxas...BOOM!...accused him of collaboration with the British, required him to surrender an unspecified number of strategic points by dawn or else face the consequences... CRASH!

Later, Mussolini's son-in-law, Count Ciano, would point out that the ultimatum left no way out for Greece: 'Either she accepts occupation or she will be attacked.' Metaxas, renowned for his past refusals to offer Mussolini any excuse for war, had little choice: 'In three hours, I could not set my own house in order, much less surrender my country. The answer is no.'

The Italian air offensive did not break Greek morale as anticipated. Warnings to Mussolini about the lack of preparation in Albania proved dreadfully correct. BOOM! Italian troops failed to make a decisive breakthrough and their supply system began to collapse in harsh winter conditions of rain and snow. BOOM! BOOM! The situation for these troops became 'nightmarish...shells caused horrible wounds; field hospitals, bandages, lint, drugs were lacking. The wounded were tended under lorry tarpaulins or in the debris of cottages. Uniforms were tattered, thread broke at the seams, cloth turned out as hard as parchment and weighed heavily without providing warmth or protection.' The Greek counter-attack launched in mid-November drove the Italians back into Albania and: 'The small, untidy Greek soldier had performed a miracle. What was intended to be murder now looked like suicide.'

Then the British became involved. And Hitler became infuriated... BOOM...CRRRASH! He realised that his Italian ally was turning into more of a hindrance than a help (as highlighted last November at Taranto when devastation caused by the planes of British aircraft carriers upon large Italian warships revealed the superiority of naval aviation over the guns of battleships) and that something had to be done. In a mere matter of weeks Hitler's troops managed to achieve the quick and decisive action that had eluded the Italians for months. As the Nazis tore through the Balkans, initial Greek defiance was urged by King George the Second who wrote:

'Greeks! A new enemy this morning insulted the honour of our country. With no warning, at the same moment as the German government handed the Greek government a document simply announcing their action, German troops attacked our frontiers. Our heroic army, watchful guardian of the sacred soil of our country, is already defending it with its blood.

'Greeks! The Greek people, who have proved to the world that they rank honour above everything else, will defend it against this new enemy to the end. Attacked today by yet another empire, Greece, so small, is at the same time so great that she will allow no-one to touch her. Our struggle will be hard and without mercy. We shall not be afraid. We shall bear all our sufferings and shall not shrink from any sacrifice, but victory is waiting for us at the end of the road to crown Greece once again and for all time...forward, children of Hellas, for the supreme struggle for your altars and your hearths! George II.'

Sadly, however, this rhetoric proved ineffective, Greek resistance collapsed, and the evacuation of Allied forces became inevitable.

Lieutenant Sutton peeps above the parapet of his trench. Is there a lull in the bombing? The Messerschmitts appear to have turned due north. As he tries to assess the damage, he notes how the attacks have been concentrated against anti-aircraft gun positions and the now-deserted aircraft pens around the airfield. It looks, he reckons, as if damage to the Royal Air Force camp area may not be as bad as anticipated. He stares up towards Hill 107 and beyond. Everything seems abandoned, withdrawn. This, of course, has to be expected and matters should remain that way until the 'all clear' has been sounded.

His gaze follows a dry river bed that twists its way through boulders, trees, vineyards, olive groves, scrub. Higher up he spots bleak gorges that lead ever deeper into complexes of mountains. These form part of the White Mountains of Western Crete, in places over 8,000 feet high. He peers through surrounding heat haze to observe the barren ranges, dead-looking, lacerated by landslides. Habitation is sparse and life is harsh within those areas of solitary villages, isolated shepherd's huts, scattered herds of goats. The clinks of bells that normally reveal the herds' presence should be absent just now: presumably the goats will have taken refuge along with every other living creature.

He squints against the sun as he continues to scrutinise the mountains to the west and due south of him. He ponders the Spartan existence of those who reside there and the way their lives have been influenced by centuries of tradition. He pictures the villages with their characteristic houses, generally small, often just a single room with a beaten earth floor spanned by archways to support rough-hewn beams and planks.

A typical Cretan roof will be formed by fresh layers of trodden earth pierced by precarious placements of modified amphoras designed to create a chimney-pot for the ancient hearth below. Perhaps the walls, blackened near the hearth, will be decorated with strings of onions and dried tomatoes, a wooden mule saddle and bridle, maybe an icon or two. Furniture may consist of a few rush-bottomed chairs, a battered table, a rickety loom. At night, while whole families sleep end to end under well-worn blankets and homespun capes, they will be joined by hens free to peck their way in and out. In daylight hours, signs of life will be found near springs as women thump and rinse their laundry then spread the garments across boulders to dry in the sun.

He knows that the villages have been constructed in carefully-selected places below ridge lines. The inhabitants have been taught by fathers and grandfathers on the need to retreat uphill in order to gain advantage over attackers, and to fire on them from above. He realises that the Cretans are born irregular fighters, well accustomed to insurrections and bloody reprisals. The populace, after all, has been compelled to endure three centuries of Turkish occupation which ended only a few years before the outbreak of World War One. Before the Turks, the island was under the Venetian suzerainty, before that the Byzantine Empire.

Cretans have become used to a state of endless revolt. They have learned to fight savagely for their independence and their warlike habits have engendered free spirits, a sense of burning nationalism, and a fiery determination to resist occupation at any sacrifice. In the wilder regions, people have become geared to lawlessness; the desolate nature of the countryside has put many beyond the reach of the law. The use of guns has become an accepted part of mountain life and most shepherds will be armed. The toughest, most intransigent attitudes will be found in the remotest, rockiest and poorest areas of the island.

The mountain dwellers show benevolent hospitality to those they see as friends. The lieutenant is aware of the Cretan penchant for fun and festivity; little excuse would be needed for grinning locals to hand out glasses of Crete's fiery spirit, *tsikoudia* or raki, with bowls of walnuts and olives to help disperse the high alcoholic content.

At Cretan dances, evidently every bit as energetic as Scottish ceilidhs, floors would thump, limbs would fly, and voices would scream as dancers flung themselves into *mantinades*, the improvised couplets relished by Cretans. The lieutenant has heard of the habit of young Cretan men (even, on occasions, those not so young) to pull pistols, empty the bullets into the rafters (an aspect, one assumes, unlike a Scottish ceilidh) all the while yelling exuberant approval at the accelerating scrape of a bow against the triple strings of a *lyra*.

Unfortunately, the lieutenant and his fellow officers lack opportunities to sample these friendly celebrations at first hand. Over the coming days, Allied troops become involved in life-and-death efforts to escape the Germans, and will learn that the diverse Cretan landscape can be far from friendly. Despondent Allied troops, tortured by hunger and thirst, will be obliged to scramble up and down treacherous rocks and landslides, traverse massifs and canyons, cross jagged peaks of mountains, negotiate crags and sheer formations inclined to induce vertigo.

The landscape's rugged nature will seem to expand the island to an area many times its actual size. Men will be forced to cover large stretches devoid of habitation, apart from roaming goat herds and wild shepherds. The men will stumble across villages and passing travellers, otherwise they will find scant respite as they aim to reach the island's south coast. Once there, they will discover a region where the land falls sheer into the sea and where widely-separated villages and hamlets, some hardly more than settlements, provide little refuge except for *caiques* and other vessels that ply the eastern seas of the Mediterranean.

This, though, lies a few days in the future. Just now, as a developing hubbub from others in the trench prompts him to revert his gaze from the mountains, the lieutenant spots men shifting their positions in the trench. Some make attempts to stand up. The petty officer orders them to keep down, but his voice suddenly falls quiet as everyone listens to the steady sound of the all-clear bell.

23

Know Thy Enemy

Lieutenant Sutton climbs out of his trench, brushes himself down, and then resumes his journey towards the operations set-up. Soon, as he meets up with other officers, he steps into the operations hut where all will be given a current appraisal of the threat posed by German forces now amassed at Greek ports. An invasion of Crete appears imminent and officers will receive the latest intelligence data on seaborne and airborne forces, including paratroopers, expected to be used by the enemy.

When the briefing begins, the intelligence officer stresses that information has been gleaned largely through lax German wireless discipline (the input of Ultra will remain secret for many years yet). The officer reveals current estimates of the size of German forces in Greece and he points out that as a precursor to invasion, further air raids can be expected throughout the day. Meanwhile, defensive positions should be inspected and improvements made with special emphasis on the need for effective camouflage and concealment.

The briefing does not take long but before officers disperse, the intelligence officer advises those present to acquaint themselves, on the basis of 'know thy enemy', with updated information contained in files on the modus operandi and other aspects of German airborne troops.

Lieutenant Sutton picks up a particular file. He flicks through the pages, then pauses at an item which examines the background to Hitler's airborne troops, a military arm regarded by the *Führer* as one of his most secret of weapons. The leader of the Nazi airborne troopers, General Kurt Student, is depicted as a bold officer whose ideas sometimes conflict with those of more cautious and conservative colleagues. General Student combines meticulous staff work and attention to detail with an 'inclination to the new, the unconventional, even the adventurous'.

Student's high-pitched voice and modest bearing could give the impression of mediocrity, and an accident last year has left him slow of speech. However, this handicap, sometimes mistaken for simple-mindedness (one of his fellow officers, General Meindl, has described him as 'a man with big ideas but not the faintest conception as to how they were to be carried out'), should not obscure the fact that General Student is a ruthless individual and a formidable opponent. He is known to be calm in a crisis, and popular with his men who appreciate his rough and ready sense of humour.

The lieutenant reads how Student's men were encouraged to adopt the 'parachutist's spirit' and to regard themselves as exceptional soldiers, superior to others. The 'old sweat type' recognised by soldiers the world over – the hard-drinking, hard-fighting individual – always in trouble in peacetime, always in the defaulters book but still a boon on the battlefield, did not fit the elitist image required.

Nazi propaganda exploited well-known personalities in the Parachute Division, for example the champion boxer Max Schmeling, a popular hero in Germany. In January 1941, when the Luftwaffe journal *Der Adler* featured an article about Schmeling, pictures showed him helping members of his platoon to adjust their parachutes before he led the jump from a Junkers Ju 52. The subtext declared that it was natural for a man like Schmeling, 'a fighter by nature' to 'take his stand in the very front line in Greater Germany's struggle for existence'. In German cinemas, audiences were treated to dramatic footage that featured 'the tough training of bronzed and muscular *Herrenvolk* (master race) at parachute school'. In the cafes of garrison towns, girls vied to associate themselves with these elite men whose badge revealed the golden plunging eagle, 'symbol of a new and glamorous type of warfare'.

Intelligence reports have suggested that three out of four of those who applied to join the German parachute forces failed to reach General Student's exacting physical and psychological standards. Their training, which began with a jump from a tower, ended with a mass drop from 400 feet under simulated battle conditions. All recruits had to go through the same training regime regardless of rank, a system designed to stimulate a sense of discipline based on mutual respect.

To set an example to their troops, the senior ranks would jump first, and the enlisted men last. Officers, therefore, would reach the ground ahead of the men and thus be in a position to rally the rest of the 'stick'. Every volunteer had to learn the code of paratroopers, the so-called ten commandments, which emphasised the need for physical fitness, comradeship, and unlimited fighting spirit. The ethos stemmed from the Hitler Youth movement from where many of the men were recruited. Churchill himself described the paratroopers as: 'the flame of the Hitler

Youth movement...an ardent embodiment of the Teutonic spirit of revenge for the defeat of 1918.' In recruiting drives, the Parachute Division would take advantage of this 'Teutonic spirit'.

The parachute troops would be taken into battle by the three-engined Junkers Ju 52, an aircraft developed as an airliner in the 1920s. The machines, stripped of much of the normal gear inside the fuselage, were fitted with canvas seats for thirteen paratroopers. Equipment could be carried in bomb racks under the wings. A staffel of Ju 52s could carry a company of 156 paratroops. Some fifty aircraft were needed to transport an entire reinforced regiment. In addition to their paradropping role, the Ju 52s could be used to tow gliders loaded with troops and equipment. As a tug, the Ju 52 could pull a single DFS 230, a rugged glider with a shallow gliding angle and a good lift-to-weight ratio. The glider could carry eight men sitting astride a narrow bench along the fuselage.

The DFS 230, which could cruise fifty or so miles after release at 15,000 feet, had a strong fixed undercarriage suitable for air landing operations in rough terrain. General Student had recruited famous glider pilots, including a world champion, into his gliding school and his troops were incorporated into a special assault regiment. The general's tactics envisaged gliders swooping silently from the sky to take the enemy by surprise. This would pave the way for the parachute forces that followed. Student's theories, however, came under severe test in 1940 when his troops suffered heavy losses in Holland and Belgium.

The lieutenant now reads about the design of German parachutes. It seems that a number of technical problems remain despite recent improvements. Following the parachutist's jump, the half-globe of his parachute canopy is designed to be opened automatically by a static line hooked on to a steel cable inside the aircraft. In early models this arrangement caused parachute canopies to be fouled, with consequent fatalities. Although new designs have largely overcome the fault, current German parachutes still lacked shroud lines for the parachutist to pull. Held by two straps attached to his back, the parachutist would be forced to dangle helplessly in his harness with no means to guide or control his descent.

To prevent wide scattering of parachutists, German parachute operations normally would be restricted to heights of 400 feet or less, wind strengths of no greater than fourteen knots. German parachutists were trained to adopt a spread-eagled posture as they dived from the open door of a Ju 52. Although this would minimise the violent oscillations created by the jerk of the static line, the posture was hardly ideal for landing, when feet and legs should be held tightly together. Despite the issue of special jump boots and reinforced pads for knees and elbows, there have been reports of high numbers of landing injuries.

"Coming Alfie?" Lieutenant Sutton glances up. "Duty calls."

"Okay," after a last glance at his file, he now joins others who have started to disperse for the day's duties.

As anticipated, these duties will be interrupted by Luftwaffe air attacks throughout the day. By evening therefore, when he returns to his bell tent, the lieutenant will have earned a night of much-needed rest. This is the point where Brigadier Hargest will talk about his sense of dread as he contemplates the sunset over Cape Spatha.

In London, while Churchill prepares for bed, he informs his private secretary that Crete will be attacked tomorrow. As for General Freyberg, he has been made aware through Ultra that supply problems have delayed German plans. The general, as a result, has spent the last few nights fully dressed. Now he knows what to expect. He remains outwardly calm having informed Churchill that: 'Everywhere, all ranks are fit and morale is high.'

In Cretan bars, soldiers have congregated to indulge their taste for local wine. Military police have to be summoned to break up noisy parties which last into the small hours of Tuesday, 20th May 1941. By that juncture, the picture on mainland Greece is rather different as German crews clamber aboard their Junkers Ju 52s and DFS 230s. While the troopers strap themselves in, the pilots start engines, ground staff stand by, and tension increases as take-off time approaches. The Germans, though, are prepared. The scene is set. History is about to be made.

24

Invasion

The hour is still early when General Student's Junkers Ju 52s, some with DFS 230 gliders in tow, roar above the roofs of occupied Athens on the morning of 20th May 1941. The air becomes thick with the thunder of aircraft which form elements of Operation Mercury, the codename given to Germany's airborne invasion of Crete. As the city's inhabitants are awakened by the tumultuous noise, many rush into the streets to watch wave upon wave of the machines cross the sky above the Acropolis. People report that the aircraft fly low, as if heavily laden, and that some tow 'weird-looking gliders like young vultures following the parent bird from the roost'.

In a flight that will last around two hours, the men on board may have feelings of the surreal as they gaze out of aircraft windows to observe a rising sun against the backdrop of blue Aegean waters. Most of the troopers will remain anxiously aware of the passage of time as they anticipate the harsh klaxons that will signal the order to jump. At that point, defenders will become spellbound as they watch the 'gliders coming down with their quiet swish, swish, dipping down and swishing in'. After the gliders will come the 'sudden billowing of parachutes which assume the appearance of thousands of fantastic slow-motion snowflakes'.

The defenders witness the first airborne invasion in history. The situation appears 'unreal, difficult to comprehend as anything at all dangerous...against the deep blue of the early morning Cretan sky, through a framework of grey-green olive branches'. The paratroopers look like 'little jerking dolls whose billowy frocks of green, yellow, red and white had somehow blown up and become entangled in the wires that controlled them'.

While the waves of transport aircraft lumber towards Crete, Luftwaffe Messerschmitts mount an assault against Maleme airfield and the slopes of Hill 107. The initial attack, as yesterday, is timed for just after dawn. Today, however, when the first wave of Messerschmitts begin to head due north and when defenders start to think about breakfast, a second wave suddenly appears. General Freyberg, whose own breakfast is interrupted by the activity, merely grunts and remarks that the Germans are 'dead on time', a comment that means little to those not party to Ultra. As he watches the blitz through binoculars, Freyberg becomes 'enthralled by the magnitude of the operation' and for the next thirty or so minutes, defenders have to endure one of the most intense local air attacks of the Second World War.

Bofors anti-aircraft crews, already shaken by days of continuous attack, become 'almost completely unnerved and soon give up firing'. Later, Colonel Andrew will claim the attack was worse than anything he had experienced during the artillery bombardments of the First World War. Squadron Leader Howell would recall:

'The noise was indescribable. The ground shuddered under us...our eyes and mouths were full of grit. We were shaken till our teeth felt loose and we could hardly see. Debris continued to crash around us and the sides of our trench crumbled. We lost count of time.'

Caught in the midst of this chaos is Lieutenant Alan William Frank Sutton whose personal account records:

'We waited in our stand-to positions from just before dawn, the accepted routine from about the middle of May, 1941. A Luftwaffe raid appeared as anticipated, and when it was past and the sun was up, we began to disperse in order to wash and shave before breakfast. However, on this day, 20th of May 1941, we were making our way to messes when the church bell on Hill 107 suddenly began to ring out a second air raid warning.

'We had become used to a fairly brief ring of the warning bell but on this occasion it just went on ringing and ringing. We also noticed the frantic waves of men on the hillside. At once, everyone rushed to shelters and I found myself in a trench fairly near the barn which served as the officers' mess. In my trench I was joined by a few familiar faces including Colonel Andrew, Commander Beale and one or two others. We had to wait a short while, then the most intensive air attack took place.

'It was absolutely earth shattering. The equivalent, I suppose, of a World War One trench barrage in preparation for an advance on the Western Front. The whole place shuddered and juddered and reeked of explosives. Every time you tried to look up, there would be a tree whistling through the air, branches flying, debris everywhere, masses of stone and dirt, dust all over the place. The attack went on for some considerable time and when it was over, we poked our heads out of the trench to see what was happening. Out to sea as far as the horizon, we could spot mass formations of aircraft. The leading Junkers Ju 52 aircraft then started to drop parachutists and this prompted terrific activity amongst the defenders. I had my Webley .45 pistol on me but I realised that I had left my rifle in my tent. I leapt out of the trench and ran to retrieve my rifle and bandoleer. When I had done this, I ran back towards the mess but by then everybody else had disappeared. I assumed that Colonel Andrew had gone to his command position and Commander Beale to the stone hut that formed the camp headquarters.

'Left by myself on the hillside, I hurried off to find a position from where I could fire at parachutists. I ended up in an olive grove from where I could watch the parachute canopies drifting down. I witnessed fierce mêlées as the parachutists landed over defended positions. Some began to drift towards me and when they were close enough, I aimed my rifle at the parachutists' feet (I calculated that the angle of deflection would cause rifle rounds to strike the man's stomach).

'Once the parachutists had landed, I had difficulty in my standing position as the broad spread of the olive grove tree branches hindered the view. I therefore adopted a kneeling position to fire beneath the branches. One man landed very near me – a matter of just four or so yards – and I remember shooting him as he rolled to disengage himself from his parachute. (I have often been asked if I killed anyone in the war. I was probably responsible for killing many in operations, but this was the only individual that I know that I killed. Was it hard? No. It was a one to one situation; it was easy to kill a man who would have killed me without hesitation.)

'At about that stage, I heard a yell from behind me. I turned quickly to look back. I spotted a Royal Air Force fellow who was shouting and beckoning. He was outside the olive grove so I hastened away from the trees in order to join him. In next to no time, others linked up with us and before long we had formed a group of around a dozen or so men.

'We were on the lower slopes of Hill 107 and we faced the area where the main body of the enemy seemed to be gathering. Suddenly there was a shout from a section higher up the hill: "The bastards are dropping on the hillside above us! On the left!" As rapidly as possible,

I ran with my section to take up a new firing position higher up the hill. As we saw more parachutists dropping, we leapfrogged up the hill as we'd been taught by the Royal Marine and New Zealand sergeants in a practise session a few days ago. More men joined our group as we went up the hill that way, supporting each other while we moved towards the hilltop.

'Near the top of the hill we came across Royal Marine and New Zealand gun positions. Our group by then was around thirty strong so I instructed them to join up with the New Zealanders while I went ahead to reconnoitre. Hidden behind scrub, I tried to survey the area around Maleme and the airfield. I saw a German Junkers Ju 52 on the airfield and evidence of enemy activity.

'I tried to assess whether we should attempt to take out the Ju 52 with a six-inch gun pre-positioned on Hill 107, but unfortunately this proved impracticable as an Australian position blocked the line of fire. I therefore scrambled on my belly under barbed wire to rejoin my group. As I did so, a Royal Marine sergeant came running up to tell us that enemy troops were infiltrating on the other side of the hill and that we should get over there immediately.

'As fast as we could, my group and a number of others clambered over the hill to take up new positions. We were facing to the west, down a valley with a ridge ahead of us. We saw a lot of enemy activity, including a glider that landed on the ridge. As troopers tumbled out of the glider we tried to shoot them but my ex-World War One .300 rifle gave me difficulties. I had not sighted the rifle or even used it before and this was a cause of considerable regret. I was trying to snap fire at running men but I did not have a great deal of success.

'We held our new defensive positions for some hours during which period, as the sun beat down and as the temperature rose, we all became extremely thirsty. At one point we spotted a file of blue-grey coloured uniforms as men attempted to scramble up the hillside. I was pretty sure these were air force uniforms because the German troopers at that stage wore khaki overalls. Other defenders, though, were less certain and they opened fire.

'When it was realised that the uniforms were indeed air force and that German guards were forcing a number of captured Royal Air Force men to act as shields, the firing stopped and angry defenders yelled "shame" at the Germans. But it was too late: a number of Royal Air Force men had been shot by their own people.

'After this incident, German snipers started to move in. They were backed by a number of mortar units which began systematically to attack the whole of the hillside. They would work their way up and down the hill, then across, then up and down again. We could see the mortar bombs coming; it was a case of grabbing one's rifle then rolling down the hill to take up a new position out of the way of the exploding bombs.

'After a period of this routine, eventually I found myself behind a pack of discarded Royal Marine equipment: pairs of boots; a military greatcoat; and a number of backpacks. I decided to try and scoop a defensive trench in this spot. I had to make use of my Royal Air Force-issued tin hat although it was pretty tough going: the ground was hard and the tin hat made a less than perfect tool. Even so, I managed to dig a reasonable trench although, as I was digging, I began to realise that the red, white and blue of the Royal Air Force roundel on the front of the tin hat provided an ideal aiming bulls-eye for the enemy. I hastily erased the roundel which was just as well since snipers were beginning to make things very difficult.

'I found myself in a duel with a particular sniper. I knew where he was, although he had made a decoy which he hoped I would aim at. Every time he fired, I fired back. His bullets hit the Royal Marine equipment and we kept this up for some time. Eventually, as it was getting towards late afternoon and as I knew that it would become very cold overnight, I attempted to retrieve the Royal Marine greatcoat. Every time I moved, a hail of two or three bullets would hit the Royal Marine pack. In spite of this, I was able to ease the greatcoat out of its pack very slowly, although the bloody sniper thwarted my efforts to recover the boots, and I realised I would be stuck with my thin officer's shoes for my escape...

'As evening approached, the Royal Marines managed to get their anti-aircraft guns operational again and this brought down a special form of hate from the Luftwaffe. Enemy pilots launched an intense air attack against Hill 107. So powerful, in fact, that they set fire to the top of the hill: undergrowth; stores; ammunition all went up in a massive blaze. I therefore found myself pinned down between the sniper and the conflagration at the top of the hill, not a comfortable situation. However, as dusk fell, I was finally able to extricate myself under the cover of darkness. It was then that a message came round that we were to withdraw to an area further up the hillside.

'When I reached the rendezvous point, I found myself amongst a whole mass of others like me, refugees, in effect, from the battle. There were navy men, air force men, Royal Marines, and gunners all knocked out of their positions. The main New Zealand defensive positions, though, were still manned. We were given a sort of supper – bacon rolls and a cup of tea – and we swopped yarns. The general feeling was that we had done okay: this was the end of the first day and we still held the hill. As night fell, we tried to doze off, although there was no room for me in any of the trenches so I had to lie out in the open.'

This general sense that 'we had done okay' has been felt by many throughout the 5th New Zealand Brigade units responsible for the defence of the Maleme sector. Most of the men, however, remain unaware of the problems within their higher echelons.

Earlier in the day, the 21st and 23rd Battalions had dealt efficiently with the German paratroopers and there were rumours that the commander of the 23rd Battalion, Lieutenant-Colonel Leckie, had personally shot five paratroopers from his headquarters. His adjutant, Captain Orbell, shot two of the enemy 'without getting up from my packing-case desk'.

By the end of the morning, Colonel Andrew appeared satisfied that his 22nd Battalion was holding its own. He felt confident that a general counter-attack supported by tanks would enforce his immediate task of airfield defence, thereby preventing the enemy from a consolidation of its position. By the afternoon, however, Colonel Andrew came under increased pressure from German forces that had started to infiltrate the Royal Air Force camp and the southern slopes of Hill 107. The need for counter-attack was becoming urgent, but signs of implementing General Freyberg's contingency plans remained sadly lacking.

Unfortunately for Colonel Andrew, poor communications had hindered him from the battle's start. At an early stage, he had lost telephone contact with his forward companies, and heavy mortar fire had forced him to re-position his headquarters. By mid-afternoon he realised the need to execute the emergency plans to contact Colonel Leckie's position. Flags and the agreed emergency flares were used, but these signals were obscured by clouds of dust and smoke in the vicinity of Maleme. Colonel Andrew recognised that if he was to retain any semblance of control over the battle, some form of counter-attack would be required, with or without support. He resolved, therefore, to employ his own last reserves of two tanks supported by a platoon.

At around 1520 hours, the counter-attack was launched. Regretfully, the first tank withdrew when the crew discovered that the turret would not traverse and that ammunition did not fit the gun. The second tank stormed through an enemy mortar position, however the turret suddenly jammed, the machine blundered into boulders, then became stuck. The counter-attack – so short-lived – had failed.

Colonel Andrew now managed to make direct contact with Brigadier Hargest whose response, evidently, was cool. The colonel decided then that he would have to withdraw from Hill 107 until reinforcements arrived at which point a reoccupation of the hill could be attempted. Shortly before Andrew and his men moved out, however, a reinforcement company under Captain Watson appeared. The time was around 2200 hours and the captain was ordered at once to take his men to occupy Hill 107. They reached the summit of the hill without resistance, apart from one platoon which encountered a German patrol.

Watson anticipated that he would be joined by the second company, but unfortunately the dark and difficult conditions meant that the company, manned by Maoris, failed to locate Colonel Andrew's headquarters. This, it seemed, was the last straw for the colonel: enough was enough; now he would have to act. Seen from his perspective at the time, Colonel Andrew's subsequent decision no doubt appeared logical and correct. The colonel could not, presumably, have understood the full, crucial, and disastrous significance of his next command to Captain Watson.

Watson was ordered to withdraw his company from Hill 107, and to fall back with his troops on the New Zealand positions to the east. Later, some would argue that this moment was seminal, that the Allied campaign was now doomed to failure.

As the night progressed, the by-now exhausted Colonel Andrew (still shaken by the morning's savage bombing and worn out by the pressures of the day), set off for Colonel Leckie's headquarters. At 0200, when Andrew reached his fellow colonel's position, a conference was convened. It was decided not to implement General Freyberg's orders for counter-attack. Instead, existing positions would be held. The decision was confirmed by Brigadier Hargest who apparently failed to grasp the significance of committing his reserves to Hill 107 and the airfield at Maleme. Even the brigadier, it seemed, had forgotten about the policy of immediate counter-attack. Later, General Fryeburg would blame himself...

'I should have realised that some of my commanders, men from World War One, were too old to stand up to the strain of an all-out battle of the nature that eventually developed around Maleme airfield. I should have replaced the older age group with younger men who stood up much better to the physical and mental strain of a long and bitter series of battles.'

Meanwhile, as Lieutenant Sutton and his colleagues attempted to rest on the slopes of Hill 107, they could not have realised that the misjudgements of senior officers were about to set the scene for an unnecessary defeat.

Half way through the night, the lieutenant and others on Hill 107 would be woken up and told to withdraw. Not until nearly dawn, however, would the Germans discover to their astonishment that the reprieve they had needed so desperately had been granted.

Intermittent firing would turn out to be German paratroopers misidentifying the men on their own side. Of the Allied troops, there would be no signs apart from a few stragglers. Amazed German officers would learn that the slopes of Hill 107 had been abandoned by the Allied troops at one point so well placed. German officers would admit later that they 'would not have been able to withstand an energetic counter-attack in battalion strength', and that the German troopers were so short of ammunition that: 'we should have had to fight off the enemy with stones and sheath-knives.'

25

Turning Tide

In the early hours of Wednesday, 21st May 1941, at about the time when Colonel Andrew reaches Colonel Leckie's headquarters, Lieutenant Sutton is roused. He is still without shelter on the slopes of Hill 107, but exhausted after the events of the day he managed some sleep, albeit fitful and despite the fact that…

'…I was bitterly cold without any form of cover, not even a trench. When I was woken in the night, the time must have been well past midnight, two or more hours, at least. I was informed that a withdrawal had been ordered. I hastily got up, as did the others nearby. It was still dark, but as far as I could gather, I was the only airfield officer left. From the conversations going on, I learned that we had suffered considerable numbers of casualties during the fighting, that Commander Beale had been seriously wounded, as had Squadron Leader Howell…'

Later, Squadron Leader Howell would recall his experience. At the start of the invasion, when he had seen paratroopers emerging from Ju 52s, he had dashed to the area of the Royal Air Force tented camp in order to locate and destroy secret ciphers. In the process, he was attacked by enemy troopers who left him for dead. As the sun began to bear down and as he lay in a pool of blood amongst a welter of heat and flies, he started to…

'…long for water as I had never craved for anything. Some say that, faced with death, the past comes before the fading gaze in shifting scenes. I had no such experience. I was alone and dying from loss of blood and from thirst. It was a race to see which won. I only desired the race to end.'

The race did not end but another two days would lapse before he was taken to a dressing station where:

'there was a constant stream of wounded through the little door. Soon they were everywhere inside. There was no room to walk between the bodies on the floor. Darkness added horror to the scene. Men were groaning and crying out; men were bleeding and being sick over each other. The sound and the smells were indescribable. Soon we had run out of good water. Someone found a barrel of sweet Samos wine and broached it. We drank Samos and water mixed. It was just possible to get it down but everyone became intoxicated and the last vestiges of control vanished.'

Just now, as the Allied troops on Hill 107 prepare to withdraw under the cover of darkness, nearby discussions confirm Lieutenant Sutton's observations during the day:

'…German troopers use Royal Navy and Royal Air Force men as screens on a number of occasions. A lot of our men were unarmed as they had become separated from their weapons when the invasion began. If our people came out to surrender, the Germans would use them as screens while they moved on to the New Zealand positions. Our men were very roughly handled indeed. If one of them tried to make a run for it, he would be shot in the back by the Germans.

'As we got ready to withdraw from Hill 107, I gathered together quite a group of airfield personnel. As the only officer, the men would follow me. They knew me; I had been working with them at the airfield for a month. We started off in single file led by a guide who was aware of the German positions. Each man tagged on to the shoulder of the fellow in front and if we got close to a German position a whisper would go down the line… "Germans fifty yards to the right…" and we would file away.

'It was a starlit night with – as far as I can remember – very little moonlight but we could just make out the ground ahead. As we stumbled along, I found myself wondering why we had been ordered to withdraw. It seemed that we had gained the upper hand at that stage; General Freyberg's orders were quite clear and Colonel Andrew was a hard-bitten fighting man. I wondered whether the intensive bombardment at the start of the invasion – when the two of us took refuge in a trench at the RAF camp – had thrown him off balance. It puzzled me at the time and it's something I've never been able to figure out fully.

'Finally, we got past the German positions and we ended up on the coastal road which ran from Maleme to Chania. By then, a large number of men had tagged on to my file, well over 100. We marched along the coast road in two files, one on each side of the road. I led one, a sergeant led the other. We all made efforts to march smartly as it boosted our morale. After a while, we came across an Allied patrol and I ordered both files to come to a halt. The patrol leader asked me where we were going, to which I replied "Chania".

'"Like hell you are! 200 yards ahead, the Germans control the road. Turn back immediately!"

'I turned back with my men and we tried to find a battalion position we could join. We ended up moving from one battalion position to another and the situation became shambolic. Any battle is a muddle but this was a greater than average shambles. We had retreated from the positions we were meant to be holding and now we seemed lost.'

This sense of disorder is felt elsewhere, and as the afternoon proceeds, General Freyberg decides to call a conference of his senior commanders. At 1600 hours, he and four of his brigadiers meet at headquarters where they resolve, at last, to concentrate on plans for a counter-attack at Maleme. They agree that the action should be under the cover of night and Brigadier Hargest, although not present at the conference, advises that two battalions should be adequate.

Freyberg, though, does not query the use of such a small force. He is exhausted by recent pressures and he seems reluctant to question the judgement of his brigadiers. Furthermore, he is conscious of the latest Ultra message: 'among operations planned for 21st May is air landing two mountain battalions and attack Chania. Landing from echelon small ships depending on situation at sea.'

This communication (as ambiguous as the famed message of eighty-seven years ago when Lords Raglan and 'Look-on' Lucan sent Lord Cardigan's Light Brigade on its Crimean charge of calamity) is meant to warn of further build-up by air and sea around Maleme. However, Freyberg misinterprets the message as alerting him to a direct seaborne attack on Chania. This miscalculation is crucial. At this *moment critique*, with so many lives at risk, so much at stake, perhaps Freyberg should have stopped, taken a deep breath, and paused for thought. If he had asked pertinent questions, insisted on a better understanding of what was required – if, if, if. Regretfully, however, just as eighty-seven years earlier, the 'ifs' are left to fend for themselves and history would be allowed to repeat itself in a disastrous manner.

General Freyberg calculates that priority must be given to the Chania threat and that, as a consequence, the forces available for the Maleme counter-attack will have to be restricted to the two battalions recommended by Brigadier Hargest.

Supported by two tanks, the aim of the counter-attack will be to recapture Maleme airfield before dawn the next day (Thursday, 22nd May 1941) and thus prevent a further build-up of enemy forces. Plans are made to transport the battalions by truck to the start line outside Platanias, a village between Maleme and Chania. Zero hour will be one hour past midnight; this will allow five hours before the arrival of the Luftwaffe at first light. However, the journey to Platanias turns out to be protracted and hazardous, as described later by the major in charge of a group of Australians:

'German aircraft spotted us and the journey became a duel of wits between the men in the lorries and the circling pilots. It was all rather exhilarating. The aircraft had now obviously got on to us, but the road was winding along a valley and there were few straight stretches. The aircraft cruised about these straight lines waiting for us. Twice I watched a plane single us out, bank and turn to machine-gun us along the straight and I told the driver to crack it up. It then became a race to the next curve. We streaked along and I hoped the battalion was following.'

Further delays ensue and it is not until 0245 hours on 22nd May that the troops finally are assembled ready to attack. At 0330 hours, they move off. The action then becomes one of heavy fighting and stiff resistance. One officer, Lieutenant Charles Upham, will be awarded the Victoria Cross for his conduct in Crete, including his activities during the early phase of the Maleme counter-attack. His official citation will record that:

'...under heavy fire from a machine-gun nest, Lieutenant Upham advanced to close quarters with pistol and hand grenades, so demoralising the occupants that his section was able to "mop up" with ease. Another of his sections was then held up by two machine guns in a house. He went in and placed a grenade through a window, destroying the crew of one machine gun and several others. In the third case, he crawled to within fifteen yards of a machine-gun post and killed the gunners with a grenade.'

As anticipated, Messerschmitt 109s appear at dawn and then remain in the vicinity poised to attack at opportune moments. The ferocity of these attacks causes large numbers of casualties and the two Allied tanks are disabled at an early stage. As the day progresses, Luftwaffe transport aircraft continue to fly in extra troops despite intensive Allied artillery. Maleme airfield becomes littered with wrecked aircraft, and while debris piles up on the runway, the Luftwaffe pilots are obliged to search for alternative landing sites, on the beaches, across fields, or wherever an open space could be found.

Aircraft are observed to: 'career along with smashed undercarriages, shedding wings and engines while troops evacuated the still-moving aircraft as rapidly as possible to race for cover.' A German war correspondent on a Ju 52 would record that:

'Men, packs, life-jackets, and ammunition are thrown forward. For some seconds we have lost every bit of control over our bodies. Then the Ju 52 comes to a halt half standing on its head. Only two hours ago we were lying in the shade of our aircraft on the mainland and now we are being fired on from everywhere.'

In efforts to keep the airfield open, German officers resort to desperate measures. Captured Allied servicemen are forced to work on the airfield to clear the runways; if they refuse to co-operate, they are beaten or shot dead. In this way, with over 130 wrecked aircraft bulldozed from the runway, the Germans manage to fly in more transports. With growing numbers of fresh troops to commit to the battle, the Germans gain further advantage. Allied men and commanders begin to suffer from serious fatigue.

A colonel of the divisional staff would comment later that Brigadier Hargest appeared to become 'unable to think coherently'. Another officer would have to wait for half an hour to receive Hargest's orders while the brigadier tried to catch up on sleep. The slow decision making is impaired further by ongoing misjudgements and erroneous assessments.

At one point, as Hargest observes events at Maleme airfield through field glasses, he concludes that the Germans have started to evacuate in the face of his counter-attack. However, as his brigade major would report later: 'From three to four miles distant, amid dust, it would certainly appear that troops were running to board aircraft which then took off. Actually, these troops were unloading parties.' Hargest underestimates enemy strength and he lacks a proper understanding of the battle's true position. It is not until later in the afternoon that he begins to realise that his counter-attack is failing.

Meanwhile, Lieutenant Sutton and his group have spent the day attached to a New Zealand brigade headquarters. From here, he has witnessed the day's events in unexpected ways which included the sound of...

'...marching feet as a contingent of about thirty men under Lieutenant Alec Ramsay turned up. The men put on a deliberate show: they marched with arms strictly at the slope; shoulders back; heads high and when they came past, Ramsay ordered: "Eyes right!" as he saluted the brigadier. The men were then halted and dismissed while Ramsay gave an account of his experiences to the brigadier. He told how, when the invasion by parachutists began, he and his men had remained in defensive positions in their own airfield area at the east end of the runway. They had managed to hold out all day and through the night, but in the morning a very strong contingent of Germans had attacked them and forced them to retreat to the New Zealand positions along the coast. They had spent last night there, now they had been compelled to move back again.

'While Lieutenant Ramsay was giving this account, we heard the sound of more marching feet at which point another contingent of airfield men appeared. The group were under Flying Officer Crowther, an armament officer who I knew to be a very effective man. He was a tough, rough individual who was a very good fighter. As Crowther gave his version of events, he explained that he had moved up the west side of Hill 107 at the start of the invasion, just as I had moved up the east side. He had pulled together a contingent of about fifty men, and now he awaited further instructions.

'While the brigadier deliberated, the airfield personnel lingered in the area and swopped yarns. By this stage, I was the senior surviving airfield officer; all the others had been captured, injured or killed. The brigade major, Major Harding, therefore sent for me and said that the brigadier had decided that our group of non-combatants in the middle of the battle was not good for morale. The brigadier wanted us out; he would provide guides that night to take us through the German lines to Chania.

'I had a certain amount of difficulty persuading my men that this was the thing to do. They had been badly knocked about and now they felt safe in the middle of the New Zealand positions. The idea of a night march through German positions did not appeal at all. I told the men that they would have to accept this, that we had no choice in the matter and they should try to get some rest before we moved out.

'By late afternoon, however, as we were about to form up, the brigade major sent for me again. He said that the brigade's losses had been very heavy during the day, that they would have to shorten their line as a result, therefore my men were needed to provide platoons to strengthen the left and right flanks. Lieutenant Ramsay and his contingent would take the right flank down by the seashore to prevent the infiltration of Germans, while I was to take a platoon of about forty men to the left flank high up under the massif of the mountains in the foothills.

'I therefore took my platoon across country, a mile or so behind the New Zealand lines. We ended up just below the top of a knoll in the last of the foothills. Behind us there was a steep incline up into the White Mountains. Ahead of us we faced across a valley to a ridge line about half a mile away. I took over from a New Zealand officer who briefed me on the best procedure. He advised me to send out pickets into picket trenches in advance of the main defensive position of five trenches. This should be done just after sunset, and the men should be pulled back at very first light. By dawn, all defensive positions should be manned ready for a German attack. After this briefing, the New Zealand officer left with his men.'

While Lieutenant Sutton and his men duly follow this procedure, they know that the fight ahead will be hard. However, they remain unaware of the full extent of Maleme's precarious position. When General Freyberg finally grasps the true picture, he realises that a second counter-attack will be required. He sends a message to headquarters in Cairo in which he urges General Wavell to despatch an infantry brigade to Crete at once, and he warns that retreat to a shorter line will become necessary if this second counter-attack fails.

Brigadier Hargest (who by now also appreciates the true situation at last) adds to an air of growing pessimism when he declares that his troops are 'exhausted and incapable of further effort'. Freyberg's other brigadiers seem half-hearted in their support of a second counter-attack. Eventually, Brigadier Puttick declares that such an action would be 'too dangerous'. At around 1900 hours on 22nd May 1941, Puttick contacts General Freyberg by telephone to recommend the withdrawal of the 5th New Zealand Brigade to Platanias. Freyberg does not argue; in guarded language he agrees that a retreat will probably be necessary.

This must be a bitter moment for the general. He must realise that the battle for Crete is slipping from his grasp, that he now faces the prospect of six battalions being cut off. Perhaps he feels this as too awful to bear: better to preserve the New Zealand Division as a coherent fighting force capable of fighting another day.

Orders for the withdrawal are completed by 0015 hours on Friday, 23rd May 1941, and sent forward by despatch riders. The surprise of Brigadier Hargest's battalion commanders (who receive the orders just before dawn) is summed-up by Colonel Leckie: 'All were of the opinion that we could hold the position.' But it is too late. The general has made his decision. The orders have been delivered. The matter is final.

As weary Allied troops file back through olive groves and vineyards towards the village of Platanias, a sense of defeat is palpable. The men must realise that the battle's watershed has been reached. Many have seen it all before in mainland Greece; now they must go through it all again. The tide is turning, and so soon.

26

Withdrawal

While the orders for withdrawal of the 5th New Zealand Brigade to Platanias are prepared at Creforce headquarters, the night of Friday, 23rd May, proceeds without incident for Lieutenant Sutton and his platoon. Before dawn, eight volunteers who have manned the platoon's two-night picket trenches return safely to the main trench positions. However, as the day progresses, the platoon experiences difficulties and the lieutenant records that he and his men start to come under...

'...increasing pressure from enemy fire. After dawn, the Germans moved in quite close to our positions and we were subjected to continual sniper fire throughout the morning. We could see piles of Germans moving round the mountainside above us, outflanking us. I decided to go down to speak with Major Harding.

'When I located him, I told Major Harding that we were low on ammunition, that our men were very inexperienced, and that if we were attacked I reckoned we would not be able to hold our position. He said: "Just hold on!"

'I said: "We're being sniped at continually and we've hardly any ammunition left."

'He said: "Keep your heads down, keep sentries going, and just hold on!"

'I then went back to my platoon and briefed them on the major's orders. We managed to hold our positions okay and towards late afternoon I called for volunteers to bring up rations. Nobody came forward. The flight sergeant and I decided that everyone had to eat, and that the two of us therefore should go down to collect rations. We elected to follow the same route as before, a trek of about half an hour. This time, though, we were sniped at continually.

'We crawled on our stomachs but if we broke cover at all we were fired on. Eventually we opted to follow another route which took us through the next valley to the east. This worked all right and we managed to make our way down to Maleme village, and from there to the ration collection point at headquarters. We drew two sacks of rations (tinned bully beef and tins of peaches) but as we began to lug them back up to the platoon position, the clamber uphill with heavy sacks took a long time.

'This meant that it was close to sunset before we finally returned to our platoon. When we got there, I was informed that a flight lieutenant, a pilot officer and ten men had made off to try to get through to Chania. I felt very let down; I saw this as desertion in the face of the enemy.

'The unreliability of my unit was further emphasised when I called for volunteers to man the picket positions overnight. As before, though, nobody came forward. I should have been able to detail men, but I was in an awkward situation.

'As a naval officer in charge of a crowd of refugees in the middle of a battle, matters were not straightforward. I therefore told the men that I would man the right picket position myself, but as the main attacks were taking place in that area, I needed three volunteers to go with me.

'Three men now volunteered to join me, all Royal Air Force chaps. Then four others volunteered to man the left picket. By this stage, dark was falling and while we blundered about trying to locate our picket trench, we ended up very close to the enemy position. The Germans began to fire on us heavily with machine guns. The four of us hit the ground immediately, still very close to the German position. Any attempt to speak, and the Germans opened up.

'We attempted to crawl away but one of my men was wearing a Macintosh ground cape which rustled every time he moved. If he made the slightest movement, the bloody Germans opened up again with their machine gun. I put my finger to my lips, tapped the cape-wearer on the shoulder as a signal that he should unbutton his cape and discard the damn thing. When this had been done, I indicated that we had to move back.

'We found a position about 100 or so yards away and kept our picket there even though it was out in the open. This was one of the longest nights of my life. The Germans knew we were there and through the night they opened up occasionally, but we weren't hit.

'At very first light, with just the faintest of greys coming into the sky, I pulled back our picket. I was convinced that we would be attacked at dawn, and I wanted to make certain that the rest of the men in the platoon were stood-to and ready. However, when I pulled back to where I thought the platoon was positioned, I couldn't find our trenches. I knew pretty well where we were as I could see the massif of the mountains to the south and we could recognise our area of foothills.

'Nevertheless, we failed to find the rest of the platoon and we ended up on a track that wound through the foothills. We started to march along the track, still hopeful of finding the others. We had gone about half a mile or so when we heard the thump-thump-thump of marching feet. The four of us immediately slithered down into a hiding place beside the track. As the marching troops came close, I could see from the shape of their helmets that they were Allied soldiers. We therefore made ourselves known and an officer ordered us to come out. We proved our identity, then the officer informed us that his men were a platoon of New Zealand troops with orders to withdraw.

'He said that his men were the rearguard, that there was nothing between them and the enemy, so we should join up with them. I was, however, terribly anxious about the others in my platoon. It was agreed, therefore, that my three Royal Air Force men should join the New Zealanders while I should go alone to try to find the rest of my platoon. The New Zealand officer said that on no account should I follow the track; my only feasible option was to go across country to brigade headquarters to find out what had happened.

'I used to be a cross-country runner, so I went down quite quickly. When I reached the coast, I turned along the coastal road towards the brigade headquarters. There, I discovered men mustered and fallen in ready to move off. I found Major Harding and explained about my platoon, that I thought they were still in position but he said: "No. They have been ordered to withdraw."

'"Who gave them the orders?"

'"One of the Fleet Air Arm men went up."

'Nearby was Lieutenant Ramsay and his platoon, so I asked them if anyone had been up to the left flank position to tell my platoon to withdraw. The men all shook their heads and said "no". I therefore turned to Major Harding and said that in that case I would have to go up and get them out myself. The major told me that if they were still up there, on no account should I bring them down directly.

'He pointed to a map and indicated a route which followed the foothills due east towards a village by a river crossing. Having crossed the river, I was to make my way down to Chania along the coastal plain. Just before I was about to set off, a New Zealand officer noticed my naval .45 Webley revolver. He said that if I was taken by the enemy with that on me, I would be shot out of hand: the Germans considered the bullets to be of the dumdum variety.

'The officer therefore took my revolver and gave me a .38 Smith and Wesson in its place (only later did I discover that this weapon was unserviceable). In addition, I still had my rifle and four rounds. Soon, I set off at a fast pace.

'As I clambered up the foothills, I could see the New Zealand rearguard on the opposite slope making their way down to brigade headquarters. Beyond, I could just make out German helmets as they appeared over the ridge of the hill. The officer in charge of the New Zealand rearguard yelled at me to ask what I was doing. When I explained, he pointed to the German helmets and said that I had about five minutes to get to my position before the Germans took it.

'I rushed on as fast as I could, and reached my platoon's position just as the Germans were advancing up the hill towards it. The Germans were carrying their guns and searching. I located our trenches and dashed from trench to trench, checking each one individually. Suddenly, a German spotted me and began to fire on me heavily. The bullets were hitting the ground all around me and I only just managed to reach the last trench. I discovered that it was empty. I thought: "Oh God! All this effort for nothing."

'At this juncture, I scrambled away rapidly towards the brow of the hill. I was still being fired on heavily, but beyond the hilltop I was able to stand up and break into a steady run. I found a track, so I began to head along the foothills towards our defensive positions as described by Major Harding. Quite soon, there was a great surge of activity nearby. I clambered to one side of the track, and hid. I observed what turned out to be a German advance party led by motorcycles with sidecars and machine gunners. As the Germans drove past me, they were so close that I could almost have touched their helmets.

'I flattened myself against the slope, and slithered a bit higher up until I was out of sight, then set off across country. It was hard going so I steadied myself down to a 'scout' pace – running for a stretch, then walking. I had had no breakfast, so when I came across a vineyard, I picked young grapes, chewed the vine leaves and the tiny grapes, then spat them out. I got a little food that way.

'After a couple of miles or so of this, I came across a basic-looking Cretan hill village. There were clusters of huts and caves. As I approached, people appeared from one of the caves and hastily pulled me inside. There, I found a group of local folk, their eyes full of consternation as they stared at me. They gave me a hunk of rye bread and some milk which I consumed hungrily. There was conversation all around, but suddenly this turned to cries of alarm when soldiers were spotted walking towards the cave.

'At this point, everyone in the cave scattered and I was left on my own. I grabbed my rifle and took up a firing position at the mouth of the cave. As the soldiers came closer, I could see that they were Allied troops. I yelled out a challenge and told one of them to come forward to identify himself. One man did this and when I was satisfied, the others came forward too.

'They explained that they were a group of New Zealanders sent as a water collection party, but that they had been cut off by the German advance. (It was not until later that I learned that the New Zealand forces did not use water collection parties; that these men were probably deserters and that it was more than likely they would have shot me if they had lost faith in me. Fortunately, perhaps, I did not know any of this at the time.)

'After a discussion, we decided to join up. I told them about Major Harding's instructions to follow the foothills due east, so we elected to set off in that direction. The major's description of the area turned out to be very good and I was able to recognise the lay of the land. Before long, we could make out the region of the village by the river crossing he had talked about, and we began to follow a track that led towards it.

'As we came closer, however, we started to pick up distinctive V-shaped markings in the dirt. I recognised these as the footprints of a German parachutist's boots. The New Zealanders had a debate about this and concluded that they did not wish to carry on in our present direction. I argued with them. I pointed out that the footprints consisted of just one set and that surely five riflemen should be able to take on a single parachutist.

'After further discussion, eventually they agreed with me and we resumed our journey along the track. I sent two of the New Zealanders to one side, two to the other, so we could sprint from olive tree to olive tree while we advanced. As we came round a curve in the track, suddenly we spotted a group of people just ahead of us. Maybe fifty to seventy yards ahead, we could see a group of Cretans surrounding a single German parachutist.

'I raised my rifle immediately, adopted a firing position and took aim. I had the parachutist in my sights and began to apply pressure on the trigger. Just as I was about to squeeze, the Cretans spotted me. They all stood stock still and flung their arms in the air. Then the German did the same. I ordered the New Zealanders to move in and to arrest the German. They did so, and brought him back to me.

'His ankle had been broken or badly sprained from the parachute drop, so he limped along slowly. As I knew a little German from school, I interrogated him. He claimed he was on his own, and that he had not joined up with the rest of his unit. I asked him where he had been dropped, and he replied the area of the military hospital. At this, the New Zealanders wanted to shoot him out of hand. They had heard that the Germans had used the hospital's walking wounded as screens, and they thought this man should be shot as a murderer. I pointed out that the man had surrendered to me and that I wasn't going to have my prisoner shot like that.

'On reflection, I think I was wrong. Maybe I was too squeamish; perhaps I should have had him shot. Anyway, we took his hand grenades and shared them out amongst us. There was no ammunition for his rifle, so we destroyed that. As we were in no position to hold an injured prisoner, we left him with the Cretans, then pressed on towards the village. We came to the village after a fairly short time, at which point I told my New Zealanders to take cover while we sized things up.

'As a naval airman, I had been taught techniques of escape and evasion. I knew that as an evader you did not rush into situations; you took your time to make assessments. We therefore lay outside the village while we appraised what was going on. We saw a string of houses along a main street. The end house on my side was a bit detached, and we could see a woman working in the garden. This, I realised, was an ideal situation: a detached house with a woman who was likely to be sympathetic. What you had to avoid was bursting in on a group of men who may turn on you. I therefore told the New Zealanders that I planned to go for that end house. If I was not out in two minutes, they should go in ready to fight it out and to extract me.

'I stood up, and began to walk towards the house. I approached the door and was about to make my presence known when hands suddenly grabbed at me and bundled me inside. At once, I checked the ground floor rooms to confirm that there were no Germans. I then beckoned the New Zealanders to join me. Voluble discussions between the Cretans followed, after which we were passed down the street from house to house. At length, we ended up at a taverna where we found a group of about six New Zealanders. These men were eating black olives and getting very drunk on raki. We were given some raki too, and I entered into conversation with some locals who could speak English.

'There was one man who seemed to be in charge and who told me that we could not possibly get across the river in daylight as planned. The whole area was held by the Germans and our only hope was to get through at night. If I liked, he could arrange a guide. I felt very uncomfortable about this. I did not like the atmosphere in the taverna; and I was wary as the Cretans had been helping the German parachutist, and the village had a very suspicious feel. I had the impression that we were being held there, perhaps while someone went off to alert the Germans.

'My four New Zealanders, on the other hand, appeared to be quite happy to stay. They were enjoying the raki and they were loath to give up the companionship of their fellow countrymen. However, I explained my feelings and insisted that we ought to move on. After some persuasion, they agreed with reluctance. We therefore set off again and had gone a very short distance – maybe a couple of hundred yards – when we heard a shout, and saw a man running towards us. He was dashing from tree to tree in an olive grove. He yelled out that he was British. I hailed him, told him to come over.

'He was a member of the Royal Engineers and had just escaped from the Germans who controlled the river crossing. We held a discussion, after which I decided to go forward with him in order to observe for myself. I took my pistol from its holster, gave my rifle to the Royal Engineer (from this moment I was, in effect, unarmed, although naturally I didn't realise this at the time), and instructed the New Zealanders to cover us while we went forward. We used olive trees and general scrub for cover. Before long, we were able to observe a mass of Germans. There was half a company of them (probably more) in the area of the river crossing.

'After a short period of observation, we went back to brief the New Zealanders. I explained that our best plan would be to get round the flank of the Germans, and from there to make our way down into Chania. I pointed to a gully that led up into the mountains and said that we should go up there to see what was on the other side. We set off once more and after quite a way, we reached a position above a long valley below us. In the valley, large numbers of Germans were visible. There must have been at least a battalion strength held there. They had motorcars, motorcycles, mules, and horses, obviously anything the Germans had been able to requisition.

'Quickly, we retreated back to the gully before we continued our climb up towards the mountains. Quite soon, we came to an area of rolling uplands within the mountains and it was here that we spotted a Cretan traveller. He spoke a little English and I explained that we wanted to get to Chania. He replied that it would take three days to reach Chania via the mountains. At first I did not believe him. However, after a while we came across another Cretan who said exactly the same thing.

'This was bad news for us. The Allies seemed to be pulling back fast and I reckoned that we did not have three days. I realised that I would have to revise my plans. I spoke again with the Cretan and asked him if there was anywhere on the south coast where we could get hold of a boat. My new idea was to reach the south coast, then to find a boat which would help us to leapfrog behind Allied lines. He said that the only suitable place was Paleochora. I got him to write down the name in my notebook after which he agreed to act as guide for the initial part of our journey. He led our group, and as we set off, we began to ponder our new circumstances. It started to dawn on us that our situation had altered completely. Our aim to reach Chania was no longer feasible. Now we were committed to a mountain escape.'

27

Mountain Escape

The account of Lieutenant Sutton continues:

'Our Cretan guide took us to a house which was some distance from the village where we had drunk raki in the taverna. This house was quite a well-to-do one with women and children and nannies, and I guessed that it was the country residence of a well-off family from town who had decided to take refuge from the fighting.

'The family gave us refreshment of bread and wine, and while we were consuming this, I heard the New Zealanders discussing amongst themselves whether they would stay the night and have the women. I felt no strong obligation to protect the Greek women, but there was a period of at least two hours before sunset and I thought that it would be crazy to stay put. We were just above the village where everybody had seen us, and we knew that the Germans were holding in strength to the east. I tried to convince the New Zealanders of the urgent need to move away quickly.

'At about this point there was a considerable outburst of shooting from the village. The New Zealanders jumped up in alarm and I told them that this was almost certainly their friends in the taverna being rounded up by the Germans. I argued that it would be madness to stay overnight; the Germans would definitely send out a search party to find us so we should put as much distance as possible between ourselves and them.

'The New Zealanders accepted this, and before long we moved away with a guide. The next two or so hours, as we trudged through the mountains, seemed drawn out and hard going. By sunset we ended up near a ridge line where we found a walled sheep shelter. We decided to spend the night there. We huddled up against the walls for protection against the wind but I had long since discarded my bulky marine greatcoat; I had to make do with my khaki cotton drill uniform when we settled down for that bitterly cold night.

'Very early the next day (Saturday, 24th May, 1941) we started off again with our guide. He took us some distance, then handed us over to another guide. We ended up being passed from guide to guide. We were moving to the west, along the face of the mountains which was the best way to reach Paleochora (although we didn't realise this at the time). We ended up above Maleme and as we approached quite a large village, we came across a group of half-a-dozen Allied troops plus their sergeant.

'The group turned out to be Australians whose sergeant knew me from working at the airfield. He gave me a very smart salute and asked if his section could join mine. As we were thirteen personnel by now, we discussed the possibility of launching a counter-attack. We could see streams of Luftwaffe transports flying to the airfield, but soon realised that our numbers were much too small for a realistic assault. We decided, therefore, that we had little choice but to head over the mountains and make for the south coast. The sergeant told me that he had received instructions on what to do in the event of being cut off during the battle. He had been told not to make for Paleochora but to head for a small fishing village called Souyia further to the east.

'We set off once more but in no time at all heard the phut-phut-phut of a motorcycle coming up the hill. Immediately, we jumped for cover by the hillside and lay there as a German patrol drove past. The patrol went up to the top of the hill, then turned round. When the patrol was clear, we resumed our trek and began to follow a water course up to the mountain peak. We faced a day of long, hard trekking at the end of which everyone was very tired. By sunset we managed to locate a walled shelter to spend the night. This turned out to be another night of bitterly cold conditions.'

Elsewhere on the island, evidence of the enemy's growing control over events has become painfully apparent. At the steady depletion of General Freyberg's forces, there are few signs of the losses being made up. In the New Zealand Division, officers report that 'the total of killed, wounded or missing is already twenty percent of divisional strength and a much higher percentage of the strength of each fighting unit'. Platoons have moved back 'looking dazed and weary to the point of exhaustion'. Overall, the sense of 'the coming of defeat' continues to spread. General Freyberg would record later:

'At this stage I was quite clear in my own mind that the troops would not be able to last much longer against a continuation of the air attacks which they had had during the previous five days. The enemy bombing was accurate and it was only a question of time before our now-shaken troops must be driven out of the positions they occupied.'

Freyberg's choice would be stark: 'defeat in the field and capture, or withdrawal'.

Throughout the island, rumours have circulated that King George the Second of Greece has been evacuated. Later, the British military attaché would record how, at the start of the invasion, King George, his cousin Prince Peter and the Greek prime minister were awakened at dawn by Messerschmitts. The king and his entourage rushed outside to observe, and the British military attaché reported how:

'Out of the smoke of bombardment we saw a very considerable force of aircraft coming in from the north. Large gliders appeared above the house, circling round for a long time. We did not see them land, though others landed later at the bottom of the king's garden. We saw troop-carrying aircraft fly in from the west, very low and in chains of threes. Then the parachutists started to come down. We estimated that 150-200 men came down in the area where the king had been the day before. It was an extraordinary sight.

'The parachutes were red or green, and through glasses one could see the French chalk in which they were packed popping off as they came out of the containers. The parachutists seemed to come down all at once, and they descended very rapidly. We saw many that did not open and let the men fall straight to the ground. There was a great deal of machine gunning from the aircraft, and firing by our anti-aircraft units and our troops in all directions. We decided it was no use staying. With difficulty, owing to the low flying aircraft, we collected our party together.

'The whole thing happened so quickly that we could not get transport. We took to the hills, literally with what we could carry in our hands. As we ran along, we saw another party of parachutists coming down on our road. We had to climb a 1,500-foot hill in the blaze of a very hot day, and every five to ten yards we had to take cover as hundreds of aircraft were whizzing about in every direction.'

The military attaché then describes the nervousness felt when others are sighted. All around, people are anxious in case uniformed figures turn out to be parachutists; parties would engage in 'prolonged bouts of shouting before agreeing to meet up'. At about noon, when the king's party reach a cave occupied by a Cretan shepherd and his family, the party rest up for a few hours. The king and his group then press ahead for a three-day trek to the south coast and subsequent evacuation to Egypt.

For the island's population in general, however, experiences would be less favourable. In Kastelli, a port town in the north-west of Crete, Stukas attack the town before German troops, supported by anti-tank guns, advance through rubble-strewn streets. In acts of near-suicidal boldness, Greek soldiers backed by armed civilians launch a series of bayonet charges against the German troops. The Greeks suffer over two hundred casualties.

A jail in Kastelli utilised for captured Germans is struck by a bomb and the prisoners escape. When questioned by a major in charge of German mountain pioneers, the escapees say that their treatment as prisoners-of-war has been proper. In spite of this, the major claims that German parachutists have been massacred and that reprisals would be ordered. Subsequently, 200 Cretan male hostages are shot in groups of ten. One of the victims turns out to be a boy of fourteen.

In Chania, the Luftwaffe attack the city in relentless waves. Chania's narrow streets are blasted with the methodical precision of the German assault on Guernica, northern Spain during the Spanish Civil War. Messerschmitts swoop down to machine gun groups of terrified refugees who try to flee into the surrounding hills.

In the hills, groups of partisans led by priests, including the legendary Father Frantzeskakis, resist the German advance. When a reconnaissance section of German mountain pioneers reaches the summit near Floria, the lieutenant in charge despatches a motorcyclist to explore the steep, winding road that leads down to the village of Kandanos. The motorcyclist is ambushed by partisans but he manages to escape. Shortly afterwards, however, the German lieutenant's reconnaissance section is surrounded and attacked. Of the sixteen German troops in the section, fourteen are killed and two go missing. The bodies would never be found.

Early in June, the village of Kandanos is cordoned off by a large contingent of German mountain troops. The troops enter the village, work their way systematically through the area, murder the inhabitants (mainly elderly people), kill all domestic and other animals, and finally set fire to the buildings. One woman aged eighty-four is thrown alive into her burning house. On the site, the mountain troops leave a sign in Greek and German:

'In retaliation for the bestial murder of German paratroops, mountain soldiers and pioneers by men, women and children along with their priest, as well as for resisting the Greater German Reich. Kandanos was destroyed on 3-6-41. It will never be rebuilt.'

These activities would provide a foretaste of life under Nazi control described so vividly by George Psychoundakis in his book *The Cretan Runner*. A flavour of attitudes is captured early in the book:

'The Germans proved themselves to be, in every way, utter barbarians. They were avenging, they said, their slain brothers-in-arms who now filled the whole island with graveyards. But how could they justify this vengeance for their slain companions who, along with them, had tried to drive us from our homes and dishonour and kill us, and settle in our stead? What did they expect us to do? Cross our hands and surrender? This our souls forbade us to do.

'Our history too – an incorruptibly great and glorious one for many generations and thousands of years – had taught us a different lesson. No. Crete had to resist with all her might. And these strangers, strutting now in the guise of brave swashbucklers, should have been begging forgiveness for all the evil they had done to Crete; for their cruel attack upon the island and for all the barbarity that typified them; for their "vengeance", as they called it.

'Now people beheld their brothers shot with their hands tied behind them, their houses burnt and their fortunes destroyed. Children were killed in their mothers' arms, and men and women, both young and old, fell together before German bullets. Whole villages with their churches and their schools and all that was sacred, were burnt and blown up; yet they talked of a New Order. What a monstrosity!'
(Reproduced with acknowledgement to John Murray and Co.)

During the occupation, a daring abduction of a senior German officer, Major-General Karl Kreipe, is carried out by Crete's resistance organisation. When the general's car is found abandoned the day after his capture, dumped near the village of Panormo, German soldiers discover a note on the windscreen:

'This operation was conducted by an English commando aided by soldiers of the Greek Army in the Middle East, so all reprisals against civilians are unjust and in defiance of International Law. We are sorry we cannot take the motor-car with us. We shall meet again soon. Major P Leigh Fermor.'

The story, later related in the book *Ill Met by Moonlight* by W Stanley Moss, was made into a film that stars Dirk Bogarde as Major Patrick Leigh Fermor.

In 1944, when German forces withdraw from the mainland of Greece, their Crete garrison is left to its fate. The garrison retreat to the Chania area, and in the process leave a trail of destruction in which houses are burned and over 1,000 hostages shot. The garrison remains besieged by local forces until the end of the war when, before evacuation by ship from Suda Bay, the Germans have to be protected from vengeful Cretans by a large cordon of British soldiers. By then, a total of 3,474 Cretans will have fallen before Nazi firing squads.

Australian, New Zealand and British dead will be buried in the Commonwealth War Cemetery on the shores of Suda Bay. The German dead, and their monuments, will be left in scattered sites around the island. However, the Cretans, unlike many subjected to Nazi occupation, do not destroy these monuments.

Thirty or so years after the war, the bodies of the German troops (some of them hardly out of their teens when killed) will be collected from the scattered sites and re-interred on the slopes of Hill 107 with a plaque:

'In this graveyard rest 4,465 German dead from the war years 1941-1945. 3,352 of them died during the battle of Crete between 20th May and 1st June 1941 – they gave their lives for their fatherland. Their deaths should always make it our duty to preserve peace amongst nations.'

In 1947, General Student appears before a British military tribunal at Lüneburg Heath to answer eight charges of war crimes. Despite his protestations of innocence, Student is found guilty on three of the charges, although the verdict is not confirmed: the Judge Advocate Branch of the British Army of the Rhine concludes that there is insufficient evidence of Student having instigated the crimes.

The Greek government apply for Student's extradition to stand trial in Athens, but the application is unsuccessful. Student, granted a medical discharge from his prisoner-of-war status, lives to the age of eighty-eight. However, other senior German officers cited for atrocities during the Nazi occupation of Crete, General's Andrae, Bräuer and Müller, are brought to trial in Athens. General Andrae is given four life sentences for his part in the policy of reprisals. He is released in 1952. On 20th May 1947, the sixth anniversary of the invasion of Crete, Generals Bräuer and Müller are hanged.

28

Shades of Dunkirk

On Sunday, 25th May 1941, the thirteen men led by Lieutenant Sutton rise early to resume their trek through the White Mountains. The lieutenant records that the peaks in the area are…

'…of the order of 3,000-4,000 feet high. When we had set off, we followed strict march discipline: fifty minutes walking, ten minutes rest. As we proceeded, we picked wild cherries, oranges, and blueberries; when we passed cottages we were given bread and honey. The Cretans, in general, were most hospitable, many of the local folk showed genuine affection for the British. We ended up following a valley that led down to the fishing village of Souyia. As we walked into the village, we found ourselves amongst crowds of Allied refugees from the battle. However, there were not many Royal Air Force or Fleet Air Arm personnel: unlike the army, we hadn't been given orders about a rendezvous point.

'Before long, I came across an Australian army lieutenant. The two of us held a discussion and we decided that the present unsatisfactory set-up should be properly organised. We therefore gathered together all the non-commissioned officers and put them in charge of platoons. These platoons were detailed in turn to guard the approaches to the village. I reckoned that if my group could march unchallenged into the village, so could the Germans.

'We appointed one of the non-commissioned officers as quartermaster, and told him to go round the men to collect any money. The money was handed over so that the quartermaster could go into the local area to buy up food. He bought bread, honey, eggs, sacks of potatoes, vegetables, and a calf which the New Zealanders slaughtered to make beef stew. This was successful, and by nightfall we had managed to feed everybody. We spent the night sleeping down by the water edge while a platoon guarded us.

'The next morning, when we were having breakfast, I was called to the telephone. The island's telephone system at that stage was working in certain areas, including the south coast. A man spoke to me and said he was Lieutenant Blake RNR in charge of the Royal Navy motor launch ML 1011 which had been sunk by enemy action off Paleochora. I told him that his best idea would be to join me at Souyia, but in view of the lack of transport, he and his crew would have to walk. They arrived that afternoon, quite tired and shaken.

'Lieutenant Blake told me that they had been attacked while in the process of taking a mobile radio station and signals books to Sphakia, a coastal village about twenty miles to the east of Souyia. This was the first time I had heard of Sphakia. Up to that point, I had envisaged that the Allies still held the northern plains, and that my main objective should be to get back behind the British lines there. Now I was being told that an Allied evacuation was under way at Sphakia.

'We concluded, therefore, that a move there would be our best plan. The Australian army lieutenant said that he would come, as did my group of Australians from the airfield, but the New Zealanders said they would stay. They claimed they were too knocked about, and they couldn't face any more mountain climbing. We then searched for a Cretan guide before setting off.

'I had hoped to reach Sphakia by dawn, but the journey proved far too gruelling. Individuals had to grasp at rocks, pull themselves up the mountainside, then crawl along slowly. The process was much harder than expected and eventually we were forced to seek rest. We opted to sleep out in the open, quite near the tops of the mountains.

'The next day, the group started off again before first light but at dawn we became aware of German aircraft. The Luftwaffe had decided to operate reconnaissance machines accompanied by Ju 88s and Me 110s higher up. These aircraft would patrol the passes then attack anything that was seen. At this stage in the day, with the sun still low in the sky, any shadow seemed enormous.

'I briefed my men, therefore, that on the cry: "aircraft!" they were to halt immediately, crouch down low to look like a rock, and remove any conspicuous-looking headgear. On no account was anyone to stare up. As a naval observer, I knew that if people looked up, they were much more likely to be spotted. Once the aircraft were clear, I would give the command "go on" and in this manner we managed to move forward in a series of rushes.

'The journey took us pretty much all day. The landscape was

covered in boulders, and there was quite a lot of snow even though it was late May. My regulation officers' black shoes were cut to pieces; I was left with virtually no soles. By the day's end we faced a long flog down a very steep ravine as we headed towards a tiny fishing village.

'When there, we made contact with local people who told us that we were still some way from Sphakia. Arrangements were made, therefore, for a Greek *caique* to pick us up after dark. This boat, manned by a British crew, turned out to be one of the boats used to gather intelligence around the Ionian Sea and the Aegean Islands. We were taken to Sphakia as planned and once there I was summonsed to see a colonel of artillery.

'This officer was in a bad way. In fact, he was in a terrible state. He had been bomb blasted and he was bleeding from his nose, eyes, ears and mouth. He looked as if he had been absolutely knocked to hell. (I learned later that he survived, but that one of his legs had to be amputated. I retain vivid memories of this army officer who, despite the severity of his wounds, remained staunchly determined to carry out his duties.)

'He asked me who I was. I explained that I was a naval lieutenant from Maleme. He said: "Right! There is to be an evacuation from here and I want you to take over. I need medical treatment. You must take over." Before he left, I asked one or two questions but the colonel said that he knew very little. He thought that destroyers would be sent tonight or tomorrow night to pick men up, but that was about all he knew.

'When the colonel had left, I set about surveying the beaches. The village was set in a cove with a small shingle beach to the western side which I estimated had sufficient room to land boats. From my days on destroyers, I reckoned that about four boats could operate from the beach landing points, then take men to ships in the bay. Having decided on the beach landing points, I requisitioned equipment to mark them.

'By use of biscuit tins, paraffin lamps, and wooden posts of various description, I worked out arrangements of markers (albeit Heath Robinson) which were hidden from Luftwaffe aircraft above, nevertheless visible to a boat from seaward. On the headland, I fixed up more markers so the boats would have a line to steer. I was helped by soldiers, one of whom asked me how the Greek word *caique* was pronounced. I replied: "As in 'cake', I believe." He reflected for a moment, then grinned:

'"But I thought you couldn't have your *caique* and eat it."

171

'I was, however, in no particular mood for humour and the feeling was strengthened when I went to speak with the captain who had picked us up at Souyia. I told him there was a party of 150 to 200 men still at Souyia and that we had to go back there to rescue them. The captain, though, said that the distance was too great and he would not go. I therefore decided to requisition one of the *caiques* lying off the beach.

'I spoke to the crew of the motor launch whose officer (Lieutenant Blake) had telephoned me at Souyia the day before. However, he said that on no account would his crew go. I replied that I wasn't asking him to go; I would take command myself, but I needed his crew. He said that he couldn't advise them to go as they had been through too much already. At that point, I appealed directly to the crew. I asked if anyone was willing to come with me, but nobody offered.

'I began to get very angry; I started to pull my revolver but thought better of it. I spoke to the men again. I said that I wanted the motorman and the stoker to step forward. They did. I asked them if they were prepared to come with me. "Yes." I asked the coxswain the same question. "Yes." I wanted one seaman to step forward. A man did. Will you come? "Yes." My Australians, who by now were adhered to me firmly, offered to come too and in this way I managed to concoct a scratch crew.

'We tried to get one of the boats out to sea but discovered there was no diesel fuel. We scavenged around locally but it had all been concealed (very sensibly). We asked locals for assistance but they claimed they didn't know where it had been hidden. Regretfully, I then had to abandon my idea of a rescue mission to Souyia. I concentrated instead on rechecking preparations for the arrival of destroyers at Sphakia. Men were briefed on how to light the markers when ordered to do so, and we spent the rest of the night waiting for the destroyers to come. But we waited in vain. None came.'

While the men at Sphakia waited for destroyers, elsewhere on Crete there have been developing signs of discipline breakdown amongst the Allies. Rumours of a withdrawal have spread, and roads into the mountains have become crowded with leaderless men and deserters. As Allied command and control arrangements begin to collapse, General Freyberg presses General Wavell in Alexandria for authority to proceed with an evacuation. Later, Freyberg would describe the 'disorganised rabble' that had commenced on the trek south: 'Somehow or other the word about Sphakia had got out and many of these people had taken a flying start in any available transport they could steal.'

By mid-afternoon on Tuesday, 27th May 1941, General Wavell (unable to gain authorisation from London where Churchill seems reluctant to admit defeat) acts on his own authority to approve a withdrawal to Sphakia. London is informed, and later in the day Churchill reports to his War Cabinet that: '...all prospects of winning the battle in Crete now appear to have gone and we have to face the prospect of the loss of most of our forces there.'

Exactly one week has elapsed since the start of the German invasion.

29

Final Scenes

At around first light on Wednesday, 28th May, Lieutenant Sutton becomes aware of large numbers of Allied troops streaming towards Sphakia. These are exhausted men, half-starved, afflicted by an air of defeat after desperate trudges across the mountains. Men have witnessed gruesome scenes: corpses left to rot; wrecked vehicles abandoned in haste along with weapons, equipment – cooking pots, ammunition, boots, helmets, items of uniform – and personal mementoes. Tracks and mountain passes have become strewn with the flotsam of an army in rout.

Men would record a 'cruel culmination to a battle that had ended in defeat', and that they had passed fields…'sprinkled with the deceased… we saw a paratrooper, still attached to his parachute, hanging from the telephone wires. Half his head had been blown off.' Many of the Allied troops would end up 'literally walking in their sleep, not even conscious that they were still moving, senses dead to all about them'.

Combat units have maintained their discipline, but these troops have had to push their way through crowds of stragglers, deserters, and general renegades. Disorganised men from base units have become frantic in their efforts to reach the safety of the south coast. One New Zealander would recollect the scene around a well surrounded by:

'…Greeks, Aussies, Tommies, N. Zeders, all mad with thirst and I have never seen such a terrible and raving crazy mob. Rifle pull-throughs, and anything in the shape of a string, were joined together to make a rope upon which tins, hats or anything that would hold water was tied and used to drag water from the well.'

On the approaches to Sphakia, a group of armed Cretan women offer food and wine in exchange for weapons. "If there is any one of you who can no longer carry his gun," yell the women, "he should either destroy it or hand it over to us so that the Germans don't get their hands on it. Tomorrow we'll need it again. The battle has not ended for us."

As this grim scenario develops, General Freyberg vacates his headquarters in the north of the island. He retreats to a cave near the Imbros Gorge from where he oversees the Allied evacuation. Major-General Weston takes command of the fighting troops who will act as rearguard supported by a light tank to block the German advance towards Sphakia.

Meanwhile, Lieutenant Sutton is joined at the beach-head at Sphakia by…

'the naval officer formerly in charge at Suda Bay, Rear-Admiral Morse, and his staff. I went round the beach-head area with the admiral's staff officer, Commander Wauchope, who approved all of my arrangements. I was then detailed to act as the beach-master and informed that, unlike last night, tonight we could expect the destroyers to appear. This was anticipated in an atmosphere of considerable apprehension as the hours ticked by. Eventually, at around midnight, we began to pick up the distinctive hum of destroyer turbines in the distance to seaward. It was an emotive moment. We realised that, after all, we were about to be rescued by Royal Navy destroyers.

'Boats from the three destroyers came ashore and I was terribly anxious to see that people were down on the beach, lined up and ready to be embarked as soon as the boats touched the shore. Unfortunately, the brigadier in command of the army's beach-head had very different ideas to my own. I urged on him the need for speed and I said that we ought to have queues of men lined up Dunkirk-style. But he insisted that he wasn't going to have his men congregated in lines liable to be shot up by the Germans.

'I explained that the Germans had not advanced as far as that, but he refused to be persuaded. As a result, the atmosphere between the two of us became very bad tempered and the evacuation went ahead very slowly indeed. That first night we got off about 800 people, mainly wounded which meant, of course, further delays as we manhandled stretchers.'

As dawn approaches, embarkation is terminated and the three destroyers set off for Alexandria at maximum speed. En-route they are attacked by four Ju 88s, nonetheless the ships manage to reach port without loss. Matters, though, are different for a force of destroyers and cruisers that have evacuated some 4,000 men from Heraklion. This force is attacked by

Stukas and by the time the ships limp into harbour at Alexandria, over twenty percent of the embarked troops have been killed or wounded. The arrival of the bomb-damaged vessels is witnessed by Admiral Cunningham who later recalls that he could '...never forget the sight of those ships coming up harbour, the guns of their fore-turrets awry and the marks of their ordeal only too plainly visible'.

Further evacuation from Sphakia is planned and while the ships are anticipated at night, waiting troops remain on tenterhooks during the day. As men listen to the distant guns of the rearguard, individuals speculate on their chances of rescue. While the evacuation by ship proceeds, General Freyberg is ordered out by Sunderland flying boat. The general agonises about having to leave his men. He is, however, given no choice as his capture might compromise Ultra. Before handing over command to Major-General Weston, Freyberg sends a last signal to General Wavell: 'I am in despair about getting these British, New Zealand and Australian units off who have fought most gallantly in the rearguard. Do your best for us. Send one last lift tomorrow night. We could embark anything up to 7,000.'

While the troops file down to the Sphakia beach-head, they are jostled by crowds who try to push their way into the slow-moving columns. One New Zealand soldier later recollects how:

> '...you had to keep your hand on the man in front of you, on his shoulder, so that stragglers could not break in between you. There was a register of the battalion which was read off. If there were 120 men, that was final, not 121. The last chap got chopped off and he was left there, that's all.'

A cordon of troops with fixed bayonets ring the beach to enforce order and to prevent the beach-head from becoming mobbed.

Those on the beach-head are uncertain about the time and date of the final evacuation, although men remain ever hopeful. However, at 1800 hours on the last day of May 1941, Major-General Weston is informed by General Wavell that the evacuation planned for this night will be the last. The major-general appears stunned by the news; he had expected to hold the beach-head for at least two or three more nights. Somehow the word leaks out and as rumours about the final evacuation spread, the area around Sphakia begins to seethe with increasingly desperate stragglers intent on securing a place. Brigadier Hargest would report later that:

> '...there were hundreds of loose members, members of non-fighting units and all sorts of people about. There was no formation, no order, no cohesion. It was a ghastly mess...the stragglers were the worst, as

they were lawless and fear-stricken. My mind was fixed: I had 1,100 troops, 950 of the brigade and 150 of the 20th Battalion. We had borne the burden; we were going aboard as a brigade and none would stop us.'

That evening, as a Sunderland flying boat waits to fly him to Alexandria, Major-General Weston summons one of his subordinate officers, Colonel Colvin. Colvin is told that his would be the luckless duty of surrendering to the Germans the next day. Major-General Weston hands across a scribbled order which says: '…I direct you to collect such senior officers as are available in the early hours of tomorrow and transmit these instructions to the senior of them. These orders direct this officer to make contact with the enemy and to capitulate.' Before he disappears into the night to climb aboard his flying boat, the major-general's last comment is: 'Well, gentlemen, there are one million drachmae in that suitcase, there's a bottle of gin in the corner. Goodbye, and good luck.'

A total of 3,710 troops are packed aboard the rescue ships that evening, although when anchors rise at 0300 on Sunday, 1st June 1941, over 6,500 still await rescue. An Australian major later recollects '…the greatest disappointment of all…the sound of anchor chains through the hawse. I found Colonel Walker and we sat on the edge of the stone sea wall. He told me that things were all up and that the navy had gone.' As dawn rises that morning, a discussion between Colonel Colvin and Colonel Walker reveals that the latter officer is the senior of the two. It falls to Colonel Walker, therefore, to trudge his way – white flag in hand – up a path by the Imbros Gorge. The colonel then surrenders to an Austrian officer.

Many of those left behind refuse to surrender. Typical of such men is an Australian soldier who declares: 'The bastards are not laying their hands on me. I'm for the hills.' Hundreds begin to scatter themselves within the hills, there to be hidden at great personal risk by the Cretans. If the Germans discover a family harbouring enemy soldiers, the entire family face execution. The bulk of the Allied troops, however, are captured at Sphakia and for these men the prospects of life as a prisoner-of-war seem '… stupefying, even dumbfounding…' A New Zealand soldier would comment:

'I have never felt so terribly as I did at that moment. In fact, I don't think that I had ever really felt at all till then. Any troubles I had had in the past were mere ripples compared with this tidal wave. I was deeply disappointed; I felt frustrated and shamed – above all – ashamed.'

The prisoners-of-war have to endure the trek back across the mountains to a holding camp which the Germans set up outside Chania. When they reach the camp, dubbed *Dulag Creta*, the prisoners discover unburied dead left in the olive groves and ditches around the camp. The area becomes pervaded by 'an overpowering stench, and buzzing bluebottles'. The battle may be over but the killing continues as German firing squads round up local Cretans. Those shot in acts of reprisal are buried inside the camp perimeter.

In time, the prisoners-of-war are sent from *Dulag Creta* to permanent camps in Poland, with the exception of some 800 men who, in breach of the Geneva Convention, are compelled to work at Maleme. In further blatant breaches of the Geneva Convention, those prisoners-of-war transferred to Poland are battened beneath the hatches of squalid tramp steamers with no latrines, little food or water, and no means of escape if the ship is torpedoed.

In London, Churchill is despondent. He had held out high hopes that General Freyberg's touch would ensure victory, especially when backed by inputs from Ultra. Churchill receives some consolation from the high price paid by the enemy, and in the House of Commons he is conscious of world opinion when he declares that: 'If we had given up the island without firing a shot…we should have been told that this pusillanimous flight had surrendered, to the enemy, the key of the Eastern Mediterranean.'

But the harsh reality of defeat means that during the fighting on the island 'British and Empire forces lost 1,742 dead, 1,737 wounded and 11,835 prisoners. Another 800 were killed, wounded or captured after embarking from Heraklion.'

For Lieutenant Sutton the evacuation at Sphakia has been a culmination of gruelling experiences. Assisted in his duties as beach-master by Lieutenant Bill Watts, a one-time shipmate from HMS *Illustrious*, the health of both men, as with so many, has begun to deteriorate. On the night of the 30th/31st May 1941, when the last boat is about to leave the beach-head, he is hailed by Commander Wauchope: "Lieutenant Sutton!"

"Sir?"

"You can leave on this boat. You can go now."

At this, the lieutenant calls across to his assistant beach-master: "Bill!"

"Alfie?"

"We're off. We've been told to go. Hurry, or we'll be left behind. Climb aboard."

When the landing craft pulls away from the beach-head to make for the destroyer HMS *Napier*, Lieutenant Sutton later recalls that '…as we went up over the ship's side, the officer of the watch, a warrant officer, stopped me at the top of the gangway. He pointed to my pistol holster and asked: "Is that pistol loaded?"

'"Of course it's loaded. I've been fighting Germans. What do you expect?"

'"Don't you know that it's forbidden to embark with a loaded pistol?"

'"Yes. As a matter of fact, I do know. I'm terribly sorry. I'm a naval officer and I apologise for the mistake."

'"You're a naval officer?"

'"Yes. I'm a lieutenant."

'"Oh," the warrant officer paused. "In that case, sir, come with me, please."

'The warrant officer then took me to his own cabin which he handed over for the entire trip.'

Shortly after dawn, when two Ju 88s 'swooped out of the sun' to attack HMS *Napier*, 'a brain-shattering din broke out as every gun and every rifle on the ship went into action'. One bomb, having shot beneath the ship's rail, explodes alongside. The resultant eruption drenches the men on deck and damages the engine room. Below decks, a New Zealand colonel in the middle of shaving would recall…'a stunning concussion… everything loose in the cabin crashed all ways and I found myself sitting on the floor in darkness. My first thought was that the cable announcing my safe arrival would not now be sent.'

While HMS *Napier* lies dead in the water, the crew struggle to repair the ship. A renewed attack is expected and tensions remain high. Later, though, men will learn that the anticipated further attack fails to materialise as Luftwaffe activity has been curtailed ahead of Germany's invasion of Russia. The *Napier*'s damage control crews thus have sufficient breathing space to effect repairs to the ship which limps home on one engine

When HMS *Napier* reaches Alexandria, observers watch New Zealand troops march down the gangplank. Most of the men are clean shaven, heads held high, rifles at the carry. These soldiers have maintained their discipline to the end. As he disembarks, Lieutenant Sutton is met by an aide to the former captain of HMS *Illustrious*, now Rear-Admiral Boyd and flag officer carriers after his recent promotion. With orders to report to the rear-admiral at once, the lieutenant would remember that…

'I was in a pretty poor state. I'd been flogging over the mountains, my shoes were non-existent, I was dirty and dishevelled, my beard was tatty and I probably stank like hell. In spite of this, the rear-admiral leapt up from his chair, eased me into it and said: "My poor fellow." I remember thinking that this, indeed, was the way an admiral should treat a lieutenant.

'He then got the story out of me. He had heard from Lieutenant Ramsay's party that the last they had seen of me was charging up the side of Hill 107 to attack the German army. It was assumed that I had gone down fighting. It was an interesting version, but it wasn't quite what happened.

'The rear-admiral listened to my story with considerable sympathy after which I was sent to see the doctor. I was in quite a bad way: my hair was coming out; my teeth were all loose and I felt pretty flabby even though my muscles were as hard as iron. I was examined by a young doctor who stared at me in astonishment before he exclaimed: "I've never seen anything like this in my life. You've got scurvy. Oh my God! This is good. I've never seen such a case." In fact, in addition to the vitamin C deficiency which causes scurvy, I was suffering from a general vitamin deficiency. This was, however, rectified by a few weeks of normal living.

'After a period of recuperation, I reported to the naval air base at Dekheila, just outside Alexandria, where I was given orders to prepare my kit. I was told to report for a particular flight but I was not told where I was going. That's the sort of thing that happens in war. Security is broken if too many people know what's happening, so as a junior officer you are given no hint of what you are going to do. You just have to accept what you are given and get on with things in the right spirit.'

During the flight, when he chats with the pilot, the lieutenant will learn that his destination is to be Palestine. He will join the staff of the air officer commanding Palestine and Transjordan where his duties will entail the assignment of naval squadrons for the Allied invasion of Syria. Allied troops, including Free French units, then become involved in fierce fighting to liberate Syria from Vichy French control. At the operation's successful conclusion, the lieutenant is posted back to Egypt as naval liaison officer at Royal Air Force headquarters. During this period, he writes a report about the defence of airfields based on his experiences at Maleme. The report is passed to the highest levels, including the prime minister. Although Churchill's scrawled comments: 'reduce to one page' seem a little curt, nonetheless the report will earn its author a letter of commendation from their lordships of the Admiralty.

On 8th January 1942, a bar to Lieutenant A W F Sutton's Distinguished Service Cross is gazetted for 'gallantry, leadership and skill during the Battle of Crete'. Watched by his wife and his mother, the lieutenant attends an investiture at Buckingham Palace on 17th February 1942 to receive both of his Distinguished Service Crosses from King George V1. The lieutenant's spirit and persistence (surely as Herculean as the demands of the circumstances themselves) have culminated in a moment of pride.

In memoirs penned after the war, a squadron pilot will write these words: 'For his efforts in Crete, Sutton was awarded a bar to the Distinguished Service Cross he had earned at Taranto. In my opinion, no gong was ever more richly deserved.'

Admiral Cunningham's autobiography *A Sailor's Odyssey* will mention a number of naval officers involved with the Crete campaign, including '…the observer Lieutenant A W F Sutton. Theirs was an example of grand personal courage under the worst possible conditions, which stands out brightly in the gloom of the Cretan affair.' In the manner that seems to characterise brave men and women, the observer Lieutenant A W F Sutton's reaction would be down-to-earth. 'It was a nice way,' he would point out, 'to say goodbye.'

30

Postscript

A summary of Captain A W F 'Alfie' Sutton's life
by Captain Richard Sutton

Alan Sutton was born on 21st May 1912 to William and Madeleine Sutton. During World War One, William served with the Duke of Cornwall's Light Infantry and was killed during the first Battle of the Somme. Madeleine was left to bring up Alan and his brother, Dudley, with the help, as Alan used to put it, of a collection of kind aunts.

Early on in his life Alan demonstrated that he was going to be a survivor when, as a six-year-old boy, he caught, and recovered from, bird flu during the 1918 Spanish flu pandemic which killed so many people round the world.

He was educated at Christ's Hospital School in Horsham, a school for which he always retained a special affection. He left school aged eighteen with a First Class Matriculation in maths, physics, history, English and engineering.

He joined the Royal Navy as a special entry cadet in 1930 and trained for one year in HMS *Erebus* in Devonport. He then served as a midshipman on the battle-cruiser *Repulse* and was present when the Atlantic Fleet mutinied at Invergordon.

It was while he was serving as a lieutenant and the navigating officer of the destroyer HMS *Basilisk*, patrolling off the northern coast of Spain during the Spanish Civil War, that he found himself at a consular reception in Saint-Jean-de-Luz in southern France while the ship was taking a break in harbour. It was at this function that he met and decided to marry Mary Cazeaux de Grange, known to friends and family as Peggy. Her father ran an engineering company in Bilbao in Spain and had decided, as the fighting approached the city, to evacuate his family to France.

In 1937 Alan decided to volunteer for the naval observer branch. He qualified after a year of specialist training and so began his career with the Fleet Air Arm. It was at about this time that he acquired the nickname

'Alfie' and he was known to his colleagues throughout the navy as Alfie Sutton. During the lead up to World War Two he underwent a period of intensive flying training on Swordfish aircraft, affectionately called 'Stringbags' by their crews.

The outbreak of war in 1939 curtailed any ideas of a formal engagement and Alan and Peggy decided to marry in early 1940. Although he denied this until his death, it was well known within the family that he sent Peggy a telegram from Alexandria to her home in Bilbao asking her to join him in England and get married. The members of the two families were gathered together and the ceremony took place in Buckfast Abbey in Devon.

He served in Swordfish squadrons on board the aircraft carriers HMS *Glorious* and HMS *Illustrious*. In November 1940, flying from the *Illustrious*, he took part in the night raid on the Italian Fleet at Taranto. He and his pilot 'Tiffy' Torrens-Spence were in the leading aircraft of the last sub-flight of torpedo-attack aircraft and their target was the modern battleship *Littorio*. At that time Taranto was the most heavily-defended harbour in the world and they had to fly through the combined anti-aircraft fire of the whole Italian Fleet and all the shore batteries both on the way in for the attack and during their escape. For his actions that night Alan was awarded the Distinguished Service Cross. Richard Pike's book *Seven Seas, Nine Lives* tells the story of Alan's adventures during this first part of his naval career.

In January 1941 *Illustrious* was attacked by German dive-bombers and the blast from a bomb which detonated in the hangar sent Alan cartwheeling down a passageway leaving him bruised but otherwise uninjured. While he attended to casualties in the hangar, a second bomb-blast then knocked him unconscious. The ship was so badly damaged that it had to be sent to the United States for repairs.

The aircrew from *Illustrious* were disembarked to Egypt and, after a time, Alan became the senior observer of 815 Squadron, operating from Greece against Italian shipping in the Adriatic. He was twice mentioned in despatches for operations in the Mediterranean during 1940 and 1941. In April 1941 the Germans invaded Greece and Alan was moved to Crete and posted to the airfield at Maleme, where his adventures, and ordeals, are described here in this book.

After these operations in the Mediterranean he was appointed staff officer (air) to the admiral commanding the eastern task force in Operation Torch, the taking of Algeria and Morocco from the Vichy French in 1942. He was then air staff officer of the escort carrier HMS *Ravager* during the Battle of the Atlantic, operating against the German U-boat threat to Allied convoys. He finished the war in the rank of acting commander, being the operations officer of the fleet carrier HMS *Implacable*, operating against the Germans off Norway and then against the Japanese in the Pacific. He was awarded nine months additional seniority for meritorious war service.

It was after the Japanese surrender, at the end of the war in the Far East, that he found himself in the Philippines, locating and repatriating allied prisoners-of-war. It was from them that he caught dysentery and was sent to hospital in Australia. The after-effects on his stomach of that illness troubled him for the rest of his life.

In 1946 Alan was appointed as second-in-command of HMS *Nabcatcher*, the Royal Naval Air Station Kai Tak in Hong Kong where, among other things, he put the Japanese prisoners to work helping clear up the debris of war. In 1947 he became the deputy director of the Royal Navy and Royal Air Force Joint Anti-submarine School in Londonderry.

He was the commanding officer of the frigate HMS *Bigbury Bay* from 1951 to 1953 during which time the ship operated in the Caribbean, was deployed to the Antarctic and acted as the guard ship for the Falkland Islands. From 1954 to 1958 he was the officer in charge of the Observer and Air Signal School at the Royal Naval Air Station Culdrose in Cornwall.

After that posting he was promoted to the rank of captain and became the chief staff officer of the Aircraft Carrier Squadron from 1956 to 1958, during which time he took part in Operation Musketeer, the joint action with French forces to retake the Suez Canal. He then was appointed simultaneously Captain (Air) Mediterranean and commanding officer of the Royal Naval Air Station Hal Far in Malta from 1960 to 1962.

Alan's career ensured that he was a widely-travelled man, and this was no better illustrated than by the fact that of his and Peggy's family of two sons and three daughters, no two were born in the same country. In 1951 he purchased the family home – Northanger – a house in Munstead outside Godalming in Surrey. He kept in touch with each of his children by sending many postcards from overseas and spoiling them with foreign gifts, creating a splendidly entertaining toy cupboard by so doing.

Alan finished his naval career as director of the Royal Naval Staff College in Greenwich where he served from 1962 to 1965. He was made Naval ADC to the Queen in 1964.

On retirement from the navy, in recognition of his distinguished service, Alan was appointed to be a Commander of the British Empire. His two younger daughters went with him to witness the ceremony.

On starting a civilian career, he initially joined the chemical division of Distillers. Not long afterwards this was 'sold' to BP and he found himself working at BP's London headquarters in Green Park. He enjoyed bringing his organisational skills to his job there, although he wasn't so keen on the regular commuting journey from Godalming to London by rail. He continued working for BP until he retired in 1977.

Despite hints from the family that a move to somewhere a little smaller might be suitable for a comfortable retirement, he had decided that he was going to spend his remaining years in his home at Northanger. The bottom line was that he wanted members of the family to be able to visit whenever they desired. Certainly there was plenty to keep him occupied looking after the property, wearing out a number of lawnmowers over time, working his way through a variety of saws while keeping the woods in order (although the famous hurricane of 1987 did help to reshape things somewhat) and occasionally causing the family consternation by treating the side of the house like a naval assault course in order to get on to the roof and track down the latest leak.

He was regularly teased about hoarding things, with some justification as it turned out, for when the house was finally cleared letters and other items came to light dating from when the children were all very young.

Alan always had a very good memory and a head for facts, something that he never lost even into old age. He was able to express himself clearly on paper. He won the Admiralty Prize for Naval History in 1939, 1947, 1949 and 1956.

Alan was always a very good speaker and narrator. As a consequence, he found that a number of historians, authors, museum curators, and various members of the family were frequently asking him to recount his adventures. Among these was the author Richard Pike who visited him at his home to listen to some of his accounts at first hand.

He also remained a regular guest at a number of Royal Navy establishments for the Fleet Air Arm's annual Taranto Night Dinner, held to commemorate the battle. He was the last surviving member of the aircrew who took part in the attack, so the final eyewitness account of that famous action passed, with him, into Royal Navy history.

Alan faced his final illnesses with the same stoicism that he showed throughout his life. He died in his sleep at his home on 6th November, 2008.

Index